PEEPS AT
THE WORLD'S DOLLS

BY

H. W. CANNING-WRIGHT

CONTAINING
TWELVE PAGE ILLUSTRATIONS

Copyright © 2013 Read Books Ltd.

This book is copyright and may not be
reproduced or copied in any way without
the express permission of the publisher in writing

British Library Cataloguing-in-Publication Data
A catalogue record for this book is available from the
British Library

Dolls

A doll is a model of a human being, often used as a toy for children. Dolls have traditionally been used in magic and religious rituals throughout the world, and dolls made of materials like clay and wood have been found in the Americas, Asia, Africa and Europe. The earliest documented dolls go back to the ancient civilizations of Egypt, Greece and Rome. Such dolls – specifically used as toys for girls, with moveable limbs and clothing, were notably documented in ancient Greece, created both as rudimentary playthings, but also as elaborate art. Today's doll manufacturing has its roots in Germany though, dating back to the fifteenth century. With industrialisation and the appearance of new materials like porcelain and plastic, dolls were increasingly mass-produced, and from this point onwards, right until the present day, dolls have become increasingly popular as simple toys and expensive collectibles.

The earliest dolls were made from available materials like clay, stone, wood, bone, ivory, leather and wax. Archaeological evidence places dolls as the foremost candidate for the world's oldest toy! Wooden paddle dolls (a type of female figurine found in burials) have been discovered in Egyptian tombs which date to as early as 2000 BCE. Dolls with movable appendages and removable outfits date back to at least 200 BCE. Greek dolls were made of clay and articulated at the hips and shoulders, and there are clear stories, dating from around

100 AD that describe such dolls being used by little girls as playthings. The modern dolls predecessors, the German models, have been documented as far back as the thirteenth century, with wooden dolls dating from the fifteenth century. From this point onwards, increasingly elaborate dolls were made for Nativity scenes, especially in Italy, and dolls with detailed, fashionable clothes were sold in France from the sixteenth century.

The German and Dutch 'peg wooden dolls' (using a jointing technique where the arms and/or legs are attached to the body with pegs), were cheap and simply made and were popular toys for poorer children in Europe. Wood continued to be the dominant material for doll construction until the nineteenth century, when it became increasingly combined with other materials such as leather, wax and porcelain. This allowed for doll construction to be far more intricate. It is unknown when dolls' glass eyes first appeared, but brown was the dominant eye colour for dolls up until the Victorian era when blue eyes became more popular, inspired by Queen Victoria. Interestingly, up until the middle of the nineteenth century, European dolls were predominantly made to represent grown-ups. Childlike dolls and the later ubiquitous baby doll did not appear until the 1850s, but by the late century, childlike dolls had overtaken the market.

The earliest celebrity dolls were 'Paper dolls'; dolls usually made of cardboard like materials, with separate clothes usually held onto the dolls by folding tabs. The nineteenth century ballerina paper dolls were among the earliest celebrity dolls, and the 1930s Shirley Temple doll sold in the millions, becoming one of the most successful celebrity dolls. A similar genre of doll, 'fashion dolls', were primarily designed to be dressed, and reflect fashion trends – usually modelled after teenage girls or adult women. Contemporary fashion dolls are typically made of vinyl, the most famous example of which, is the 'Barbie doll'. Barbies were made from 1959 onwards, by the American toy company Mattel, and have dominated the market from their inception. The only doll to challenge Barbie's dominance was the 'Bratz' make, reaching forty percent of the market share in 2006.

Despite their construction for children, some dolls, such as the nineteenth century bisque dolls, made by French manufacturers such as Bru and Jumeau, may be worth over £22,000 today. Dolls have also made it into the political and artistic spheres, with artists such as Hans Bellmer, who made surrealistic dolls with interchangeable limbs in the 1930s and 1940s, in opposition to the Nazi party's idolisation of the perfect Aryan body. East Village artist Greer Lankton became famous in the 1980s for her theatrical window displays of drug addicted, anorexic and mutant dolls, reflecting the deteriorating social conditions of America's 'cultural capital.' Many books (mostly aimed at children) have also dealt with dolls, for example tales such as *Whilhelmina. The Adventures of a Dutch Doll*, by Nora Pitt-Taylor and the *Raggedy Ann* books by Johnny

Gruelle, first published in 1918. Our fascination with dolls is showing no signs of waning in the present day, and it is hoped that the reader enjoys this book.

To

ONE VIRGINIA

A GIRL OF MANY DOLLIES

THIS BOOK IS AFFECTIONATELY DEDICATED

PREFACE

In presenting this book, "Peeps at the World's Dolls," it is a great pleasure to me to think of the many girl doll-lovers into whose hands, I hope, it may come, and of the hours that they may spend in reading it and looking at the pictures. Those in colour are direct colour photographs, made by myself from the actual dolls, and they faithfully present every shade and detail exactly as these dolls appear.

Many friends have given me great assistance, and I wish to express my hearty thanks to them as well as to various books, Missionary Societies, and Reference Libraries, which have provided me with information as to costumes, customs, and curious dolls. I have also had the advantage of free access, for purposes of photography and study, to a collection of over three hundred English and foreign dolls (many of them very rare), the property of an old friend.

To one and all, my best thanks. May the book afford as much pleasure to those who read, as it has given me to write.

H. W. CANNING-WRIGHT.

CROYDON,
   July, 1922.

CONTENTS

CHAPTER		PAGE
I.	GREAT BRITAIN	1
II.	MISS AMERICA	6
III.	THE FEAST OF DOLLS	10
IV.	RUSSIA	13
V.	A FLATHEAD DOLLY	15
VI.	LAPLAND	18
VII.	ITALIAN BABINOS	21
VIII.	MARIA THERESA, OF HUNGARY	24
IX.	THE PRECIOUS CHILD OF KOREA	28
X.	SOME STRANGE DOLLS	31
XI.	LA BELLE FRANÇAISE	37
XII.	SOUTH AFRICA	41
XIII.	HARALD, THE NORWEGIAN	45
XIV.	CHANDI AND KALI	49
XV.	SWITZERLAND	53
XVI.	DOLORES, OF SUNNY SPAIN	56
XVII.	SAMOA	59
XVIII.	HOLLAND	62
XIX.	TURKEY	66
XX.	A MONGOLIAN LADY AND A MANCHU GENTLEMAN	70
XXI.	BELGIUM, THE GREAT ADVENTURE	74
XXII.	A MIDSUMMER NIGHT'S DREAM	79

LIST OF ILLUSTRATIONS

*OLD ENGLISH DOLL - - - -	*frontispiece*
	FACING PAGE
A GROUP OF JAPANESE DOLLS - - -	- 9
RUSSIAN WOODMEN DOLLS - - -	- 13
INDIAN "FLATHEAD" DOLL - - -	- 20
*ITALIAN DOLLS - - - - -	- 22
DOLLS FROM LAPLAND - - - -	- 24
HUNGARIAN DOLLS - - - -	- 27
*KOREAN DOLL - - - -	- 35
FRENCH FISHERFOLK DOLLS - - -	- 38
NORWEGIAN PEASANT DOLL - -	- 45
AN INDIAN NATIVE DOLL - - -	- 52
*MONGOLIAN DOLLS - - - -	- 70

* *These are printed in colours*

PEEPS AT THE WORLD'S DOLLS

CHAPTER I

GREAT BRITAIN

A REAL British dolly! I am to be the one that steps before you first—one of a very ancient and honourable family, and I myself am a great age, although my face is nearly as good as new and not the least bit wrinkled. One hundred years old! Just think of that! One hundred years! Long ages before your Daddy and Mummy were born I was loved and cuddled by a little girl who was Daddy's Mother, and I have been in the family ever since.

Of course, I have not been on " active service " all the while. There have been periods of many years during which I have been carefully " laid up in lavender," as they say, and put away in a dark cupboard where no one visited me at all, except once a year when spring-cleaning was being done. But between whiles I have always been the treasured plaything of some girl-child, who took great care that I was not knocked about

Peeps at the World's Dolls

or broken or left in the sun, or else I should not look so young as I do to-day. Life was very different in England when I first opened my eyes, and I wish you could have seen the funny little wrinkled old lady, and the bow-fronted shop through the small panes of which I first looked out upon the world. Stage coaches used to rattle over the cobblestone streets and pull up at the inn with the quaint sign, where they changed horses, and where the travellers dismounted to "stretch their legs." Toys were quite simple matters in those days, and I was one of the wonders of the old lady's window. A real wax doll, with a rich silk dress in the fashion of the time. Unlike dolly of to-day, my head was quite solid and I could not open nor shut my eyes, which perhaps accounts for my having seen such a lot of the world.

One day I was looking through my window, as usual, when the coach drew up at the inn, and a very charming young lady, with long ringlets, and accompanied by a gallant gentleman, stepped down and walked straight across to my shop. They did not pause at all, but the gentleman opened the door, setting the spring bell all a-jangle, and stepped back for the young lady to walk in before him. The old lady who kept the shop came bustling through from her little parlour at the back and curtsied to both as she enquired what

Great Britain

they would be pleased to want. Just imagine my surprise when they asked the price of—ME! "Oh, Richard, do let us take her!" the young lady exclaimed. "Ellen would be so very pleased!" And there and then I passed from my place in the old shop window, and became one of the family with which I have lived ever since. For Ellen, I found, was the little girl who belonged to the lady and gentleman who came to the inn, and she took great care of me until she herself was quite grown up and married.

I went through one of my long resting-times after that, and it must have been four or five years before I again saw the light of day, and quite twice that time since I had seen anything at all of the world in which I lived. Ellen, my first little mother, was married when she was about seventeen, and it was about four years earlier that she wrapped me up safely and ceased to play with me any more. And what a changed world I awoke to find when at last my former mother—now become quite a matron, and a very beautiful woman—unwrapped me and gave me to her own little girl for her very own dolly! Railways, with their shrieking whistles and loud rumbling roar, had become quite common. The old familiar stage coach, which I had seen twice a day for so many years, had almost disappeared, and life seemed to be lived quite twice as fast as I had previously

Peeps at the World's Dolls

known it. But I was very happy, and many joyous hours were spent in the sunny nursery with nurse and Katherine, until she too grew too old to play with me any more. But, although she was too old to play with me, she did not cease to care; for I was "Mother's doll," and she wrapped me away "in case," as she said with a blush, she one day had a little girl of her own. History *does* repeat itself very strangely, for, sure enough, one day I was again unwrapped, and there was the Katherine I had formerly known, a grown woman, sitting on a chair in the summer sunshine in a most wonderful garden. Sitting in her lap was a bonny little blue-eyed, fair-haired boy of about six months; while on the grass at her feet a dark-haired little girl was playing. I loved this little girl at once, for she was so remarkably like the young lady who had come into the little country shop so many, many years ago.

So far my life had been a succession of living and putting away, but never before had I been plunged into such a whirl of gaiety and bustle as accompanied this resurrection—one day here, another there; rides in what the baby brother, who soon began to talk, called the "mo-car." I was simply staggered by the change that had come over the quiet, sleepy old world I used to know. The children had so many toys that I was

Great Britain

far less thought of than used to be the case; but still, great care had to be taken with me, because I had belonged to Mother and Grandmother, and even the grandmother before that. This bit of my life was shorter, and I got put away much more quickly, for the girls seemed to outgrow their dollies much more quickly than their mothers and grandmothers did.

And then the most wonderful episode of my whole life happened. I was packed away, with a lot more toys, in a deep cupboard that never seemed to be opened, and I did not know whether it was night or day. Time passed very slowly, and I wondered if everyone had forgotten me. Sometimes I heard queer sounds that I quite failed to recognise, and which conveyed no meaning whatever to me. Among these was a most terrific thudding that used to happen, and then die away, and happen again. In the midst of one of these curious thuddings there came one far louder and more terrific than anything I had ever imagined possible. The whole house seemed to rock, and then the world around me fell to pieces. The house, the cupboard, the shelf upon which I lay, splintered to ruin. When the noise at last ceased, and things were still once more, I found myself out of doors, gazing up at the dark sky, which was filled with thousands and millions of stars. Across this black void brilliant streaks of light were moving, and right overhead they met, showing a long, thin pencil of light—a Zeppelin.

Next morning all sorts of people came, looking round the spot where my house had been, and at last one of them saw me. "What a queer old doll!" she exclaimed, and she picked me up and carried me away. To-day I am displayed in a large glass case, with all my fine clothes, and a tablet recording my honourable age. They call the place a museum, and lots and lots of the most modern little girls come to look at me, just because I am one hundred years old.

And now they tell me that I shall be better known than ever, for the other day a gentleman came and took my photograph, which is to be printed in a real book. I do hope he made me look nice.

CHAPTER II

MISS AMERICA

My name is Sadie, and I am the most wonderful doll on earth, or at least so they say. A citizen of the great United States of America, where dollies are more elaborate and perfect than anywhere else. You ought to see me when I am out with my little mistress, walking in Central Park.

"Walking!" you exclaim. Oh, yes, I can walk, just as well as you can—after I have been

Miss America

wound up. And then, I am so big too. I stand about 2½ feet high, and if you measure that out on a tape-rule by your own side, you will see how I should look if I were your own dolly. But I was telling you about my walking powers. Inside my body is placed a wonderful piece of machinery that can be wound up with a key, and when this is started, and you hold me by my hand, I can stroll along by your side, lifting each daintily booted foot exactly the same as you yourself do.

And this is just where I am different from a human child, for they have to be taught to walk, while I was able to do so right from the beginning. If you have a baby brother or sister, you will have seen Mother or Nana carefully holding them between their hands, while they scrambled along in the funniest manner. All "humans" are like that, but high-class American dollies only need to be wound up, and from their youngest days they can walk quite firmly and strongly. It is rather a funny feeling, I can tell you, the first time someone turns the key and your legs begin to step out by themselves. Of course, there are lots and lots of American dolls that cannot walk, any more than English or Chinese ones can, and these are just as much loved by the little girls to whom they belong as we are, though everyone admires me very much, and turns round to watch me as I walk by the side of my little mistress.

Peeps at the World's Dolls

Many years ago, that wonderful inventor T. A. Edison, who began life by selling papers at a railway station, invented a doll that could sing seven or eight different songs, by means of a wee gramophone placed just where my walking powers lie. She was never very popular with the girls to whom she was given, because she squeaked so much when she started to perform, and they did not love her half so well as a dolly that can take their hands and walk by their side along the roadway or round the garden.

I know something about England, because I have been there once to "summer" as we say, and I liked that very much, but, of course, I have seen a great deal more of my own country and the many wonderful things it contains. New York is not the least little bit like London, for here the city cannot spread outwards and outwards as London does, because it is practically an island, and so it has grown upwards and upwards until our buildings reach to over twenty storeys in height. Just think of that! I was surprised the first time I went into the city, because, you see, my home is right out in the country, where there is only one house here and not another for several miles.

One day we went down to the station and got on the car for the city, and after rushing along for hours and hours we found ourselves really and truly at Broadway Station. I did stare at the noise and

A GROUP OF JAPANESE DOLLS.

Miss America

the rush and bustle that surrounded me on all hands, and at the immense hotels and buildings that rose upwards in great, solid, square blocks. We were going to stay quite near to the top of one of these, and when we arrived there, we got into the lift and went up and up, until I thought we never were going to stop any more. But we did, and our hostess, Mrs. Mallison, after she had kissed my mistress, asked about me. "Her name is Sadie," said my owner, and Mrs. Mallison at once christened me afresh—"Sadie, the magnificent."

I did feel proud, too, as I took the hand of my mistress and walked across the apartment to the window, where we could look down from our dizzy height to the tiny people and cars, threading their way through the streets below us. But the most surprising thing of all was when we went out on to the roof garden. There, hundreds of feet above the earth, flowers were blooming in their pots, children were playing, grown-ups were sitting in deck chairs in the sunshine, while the great city hummed beneath. I was not long before I met one of my own sisters walking too, and before we returned to the country a fast friendship had sprung up between us, as well as between our two little owners, and the very next week that ever will be, she and Virginia (for that is my sister's name) are coming down to stay with us, so that we shall all have another jolly time.

Peeps at the World's Dolls

CHAPTER III

THE FEAST OF DOLLS

O-KU-SAN was most tremendously excited, for to-day was the Feast of Dolls, one of the many great annual festivals of Japan. She was the queerest little girl that ever you saw, so exactly like her laughing young mother that, when you looked first at one and then at the other, you might easily have thought that you were looking at the same person, only one was very little and the other a good deal bigger.

All the Japanese girls, even when they are fully grown, are much smaller than our Western ladies, so you may suppose that O-ku-San looked very small indeed, for she was only six years old.

This morning she had awakened very early, for the maidservants are always stirring very soon after it is light, and all the houses have thin paper walls, because of the earthquakes. She wanted to get up at once and begin the wonderful day, but she had to lie quite still and listen to the birds singing until the shutters on the outside of the verandah were opened and let in the sunshine. Great preparations have to be made for this Feast of Dolls, and O-ku-San wanted to be in it all and see everything that was to be seen; so, naturally,

The Feast of Dolls

she was very impatient to get to the brass basin at the corner of the verandah and be washed.

But to return to the Feast of Dolls. First of all, a platform is prepared (very often in the form of several steps), and covered with red or some other brightly coloured cloth. On this the ancestral dolls are set out in great state after they have been brought from their place of safety among the other family valuables, for the Japanese set great store by these dolls, and would not sell them for a very large sum of money. Numbers of them are hundreds of years old, and, of course, form a most interesting historical record of the dress and customs of the country in bygone days.

Often an Emperor, or Empress, or other famous personage is represented, and these dolls have to be treated in accordance with their rank. A little bowl of saké, which was brewed for the feast, is set before each one in its special pot, together with rice and numerous other Japanese dainties. O-ku-San was in the wildest state of excitement when she saw the dolls, all set out and looking so prim and stately. And what a contrast they presented, from the very oldest of all right down to the newest and most modern in up-to-date clothes!

All the little girls gazed and gazed, because, of course, they were not allowed to play with these ancestral dolls—they are only to be looked at and

Peeps at the World's Dolls

admired. If you were staying in Japan, and were quite friendly with a family, you would be gladly welcomed, with much ceremony and laughter, to their Feast of Dolls, and be taken in and shown their Dolly Exhibition with great pride. To hear their merry laughter you would think they were the most care-free and most light-hearted folk in all the wide world.

The Feast of Dolls itself only lasts for one day, but the curious mixture of old and modern dolls remains on exhibition for a week; then they are carefully packed away and taken to the strong room or box, where they remain for another twelve months, awaiting the return of the feast ere they again see the light of day. These dolls, as I said, are never played with, but O-ku-San and all the other Japanese girls do have very wonderful dolls. These dolls are exactly like their little mistresses, and, of course, always wear the funny kimonos that look so strange to us.

While they are children, the Japanese girls all wear trousers, just as if they were boys, but when they begin to grow up, these are put away and a skirt, something like that which the English girl wears, is used instead; so that you can always tell if the girl dollies are supposed to be young or older, by whether they wear trousers or skirts.

RUSSIAN WOODMEN DOLLS MADE FROM MOSS, FIR, CONES, ETC.

Russia

CHAPTER IV

RUSSIA

SUPPOSE that you had been born in that vast country which is called Russia, I wonder what kind of a dolly would have fallen to your lot ? Much, of course, would have depended upon the class in which you were born, for the mass of the people are very poor. Since the Revolution, when all the rich folks were captured or killed, or fled to other lands, there are hardly any people at all with money. But, even under these conditions, I expect that you would have had a doll of some kind, for the peasants are very ingenious people, and (during the long winter days, when the earth is covered with snow for months together) they make all sorts of different things, including toys for the children to play with.

Look at the picture of the two Russian woodmen dolls, and the curious things of which they are made: hewn out from rough blocks of wood, with painted faces, with fir cones for arms, and dressed entirely in moss, with shoes of plaited fibre. A strange pair they look, especially the one with the long beard and flat cap. One has a tiny hatchet stuck in his belt, that does not show in the photograph, but you can see the long wooden staves that

Peeps at the World's Dolls

they use to walk with. I do not think that these dolls look very "cuddly," do you? But, then, if you lived in one of the far-away small villages, you would never have seen any other kind of dolly, and so would have loved these very much indeed. The people in these villges almost all work on the land in summer, and the women and children, even quite little girls, have to work as hard as ever they can to get in the crops before the intense cold comes back again, and the country as far as you can see is buried under snow, while the rivers all freeze up.

All Russia is not like this, however, and if you had been born in one of the great cities, such as Moscow, you would have found life much easier, especially if your parents had been rich. When the cold weather came, you would have been dressed in thick furs to keep you warm, and have been driven everywhere in a sleigh. The shops were simply wonderful, and contained lovely dollies, quite as beautiful as anything that you could find in the most wonderful London shop. Here you might buy a little boy doll—Ivan for his name —dressed in a navy blue suit, with top-boots, and an overcoat very much like ours, always lined and trimmed with thick fur. For the inside short fur is used, while the collar and cuffs have long fur that buries the hands and neck in a warm and comfortable manner. Always, too, a little

Russia

round cap is worn, made of the same fur as the collar and cuffs.

If the dolly was supposed to be of the humbler peasant folk, she would be dressed in black and white with a cap, the brim of which is drawn down so far over the forehead as almost to cover the eyes. Over the dress a long, loose, shapeless black or brown coat, reaching right down to the heels, covers everything, though beneath her skirts would be long top-boots that reach almost to the knees. So, according to her rank, dolly looks in Russia, as she is cuddled and put to bed by the little peasant girl, or as she rides with her little mistress in the comfortable sleigh which glides over the frozen ice of the river near the capital at Petrograd.

CHAPTER V

A FLATHEAD DOLLY

I WONDER whatever you little girls will think of me, when you look at my picture and I tell you my name. I am sure that very, very few of you ever saw a dolly that looked the least like me before, or heard such a curious name. For I am called Skelechun, and I belong to a little girl of the Flathead tribe in North America.

Years ago, before my mistress grew old enough to be able to play with me, she used to look

Peeps at the World's Dolls

almost exactly like I do now, and her mother used to carry her about in a cradle just like the one in which you see me hanging. For really there is only my head to be seen, and all the rest is cradle, just the same as the ones in which the women carry the live children and hang them up on the trees while they work. My cradle has been made especially pretty with red, white, and blue glass beads, sewn on in a pattern; but the cradles in which the live little girls and boys are carried are usually made of wood or bark, hollowed out, and suspended with rope. Some of those who dwell inland hang bells upon these cradles, so that as the baby is carried along, or swings gently on the tree bough, the bells continually tinkle and ring.

I daresay you wonder why we are called Flatheads, and how it is that our foreheads slope back in such a peculiar manner. This is due to a very curious custom of the tribe, for when the children are quite babies their whole body is swaddled and bound up. Pads with a board are then placed across the forehead, so that it is gradually pressed flatter and flatter, and baby is laced into the wood cradle by means of a cord passed from side to side. This flattening, as you may imagine, is far from a comfortable business, especially for the girls, for their foreheads have to be much flatter than those of the boys if the young men are to think them beautiful when

A Flathead Dolly

they grow up. And yet they would feel very angry if their heads were allowed to grow in the usual way, for you cannot find a greater insult than to say, "Hoo, your mother was too lazy to flatten your head!"

I am a very happy dolly, and my little mistress loves me very much, as her father and mother do her, for all the Flatheads love their children. It is perhaps better to be a girl than a boy, for the girls are thought much more of, because when they grow up they can be sold to husbands, and a good price is obtained by the parents. While they live at home, although they have plenty of time to play and enjoy themselves, the girls have to learn all that there is to know about home-keeping, while the boys accompany their fathers and brothers on the hunting expeditions. We are a very happy family indeed, especially in summer, when food is plentiful, and Atuni, who is the father of my little mistress, often shakes his head at us both and says: "Oh, Skelechun, Skelechun, you are a bad pair, both of you."

One of the chief things we do is to make baskets which we trade in the towns for money upon which to live in winter. If you have ever seen any of the work that our family has done, you will be very surprised at its excellence and neatness. One thing I must tell you before we part, and that is how my little mistress boils water when her father or mother wants a meal. We never put a kettle over the fire and wait for the water to heat like you do. We make the fire and heat a number of stones red-hot; then these are dropped into the water, and, as they cool, picked out and more red-hot ones dropped in, and you would be very surprised if you saw how quickly our meal was ready and the water hot.

Yes, though my name is so funny, and my head so flat, I am a very happy dolly, and I hope that when Atuni sells my mistress to a husband, she will take me with her, for I know that I am very handsome indeed.

CHAPTER VI

LAPLAND

Such a funny little fat squab of a girl, with a pale yellow face that is broad and flat, sitting as near as ever she can get to the stove, for it is terribly cold—colder than you can even possibly imagine. And on her lap sits a curious little miniature of herself—her dolly. She is called Gerda, and that equally squat and tub-like little woman is her mother.

They are quite alone, for father is a fisherman and is often away for many days together, while Gerda, her mother, and I live at home in the hut. Our home is right within the Arctic Circle, and the

Lapland

whole of life is very primitive indeed compared with your land.

We are the shortest race in Europe, but very strong indeed, and many of us live to a great old age, in spite of the hard life and intense cold. The women and girls are almost always shorter than the men, and Gerda, when she is quite grown up, will not probably be much more than 4 feet tall, with very short arms and legs and tiny feet, while her eyes are set at a curious slant that reminds you of the Japanese. When you first looked at me or my mistress Gerda, I expect you would be very puzzled as to whether we were boys or girls, for in many ways we are a topsy-turvy land, and there is so little difference between the boys' and the girls' dress, that it is difficult to tell one from another. We all wear trousers, boots, and gaiters, but sometimes a woman or girl wears a few beads as an ornament, while they generally have a heavier wrapping round the head.

Our dresses are very plain, but there is generally a pointed piece of fur, cut from the head or tail of an animal, that forms a tab to finish the bottom of the front of the coat. I do not know what we should do without our warm, close-fitting hoods, for though I am only a dolly I can tell how cold it is, and poor Gerda would soon have her ears and nose frozen off if they were not thus protected. Do you notice how the women alway-

Peeps at the World's Dolls

stuff their trousers into the tops of their big boots ? If the large hoods were removed, and you could see their hair, you would find that here, too, the girls and their brothers were strangely alike. For the hair is always jet-black and worn in a straight fringe over the forehead, though it is irregular in length and plaited into two long tails at the back. In winter everyone wears fur clothes, and in summer white cotton or wool. Gerda's father, as I said, is a fisherman, so that we live near the sea in a low hut made of turf, with a few stakes to hold up the roof. We do not have any windows, because they would let in the cold in winter.

Everywhere there are dogs and reindeer, the latter being especially useful to us, for while alive we use them for riding and drawing the sleds—just as you have horses—and when dead, they give us skins for clothes. Much of my own clothing is made from reindeer skins, and if we are very short of food a reindeer is killed and eaten. Another purpose that the reindeer serves to the Laplander is providing him with milk, though this is quite different in taste to that given by the cow. If you had never been in my country before, you would have a great surprise when the winter came, for then we all shut ourselves in the hut, and Gerda plays with me most of the day; for at one time in the year it is just one long night, and it is always dark. To make up for this, we

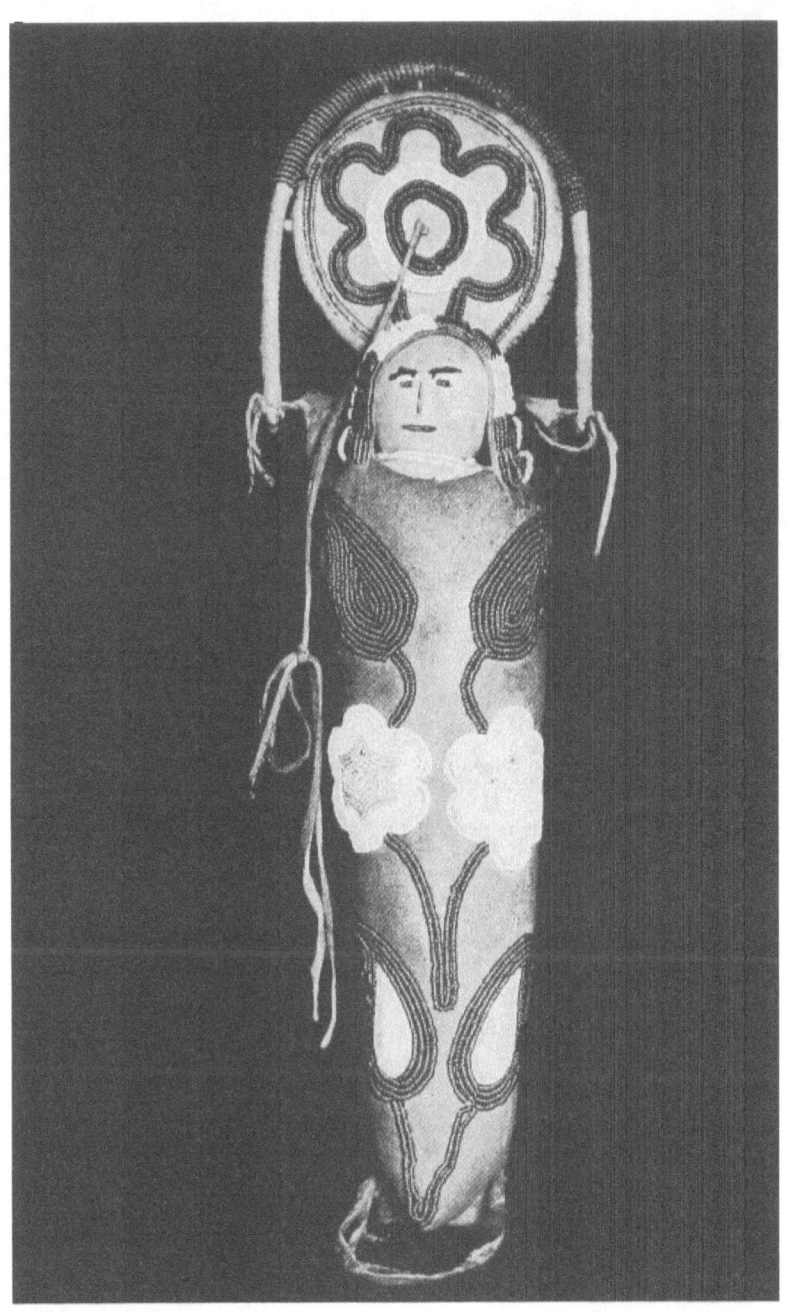

INDIAN "FLATHEAD PAPOOSE DOLL IN LEATHER CARRIER. Page 15.

Italian Babinos

have a similar time in the summer, when it is just one long day and never gets dark.

If one of your English dollies came to live with us in our country, it would take her a whole year to get used to our topsy-turvy ways and happenings, and one of the marvels that she would see is the Northern Lights. These are a strangely brilliant glow that comes and lingers in the sky, until it turns the night almost into day. But I must not stay to tell you any more, for Gerda is calling me to go to bed, and I hope she will wrap me up very warm, for it *is* cold.

CHAPTER VII
ITALIAN BABINOS

I AM a little Italian babino, born in a land that is shaped exactly like a top-boot, and my earliest recollection of life is standing in a shop window for people to come and look at me. But I did not have to wait long. One day, a lady (whom I have never seen since) came in and bought me and had me wrapped up in paper. Then she went out into the street and found a ciocciari to carry me to the place to which she had had me addressed.

These ciocciari are young girls who do somewhat the same work as English messenger boys, carrying parcels, etc., for hire. You can always tell them

Peeps at the World's Dolls

by their shoes, which, indeed, are their badge of office. These shoes are strange in shape and made from the hairy skin of some animal.

I was not long before I reached my new home, and was quickly unwrapped by a little girl, with almost black hair, large eyes, and the deep olive skin that most of us have. And how she did exclaim when she saw me lying there, waiting for her to dress me, for up till then I had no clothes to wear. She quickly gave me a name, Filomena, and, by listening, I found that her own name was Maria. Her parents were very rich indeed, and she soon made me plenty of clothes so that I could appear in public, and I always went everywhere with her.

Our land is a land of flowers and fruit and sunshine and cloudless skies, and we spend almost all our lives in the open air. I have been with Maria all over our wonderful land, and seen almost all of its many great beauties. We have been to the mountain villages, where the goats are driven into the streets in the early morning, and the people bring out their jugs, and the animals are milked as the milk is wanted. I have been among the vineyards in autumn, when the rich purple grapes were ripe, and were being picked into large baskets and tipped into tall wooden tubs called "ligoncie."

I have seen the olives picked and placed in the

ITALIAN DOLLS.

Italian Babinos

mills, where they are crushed to pulp by a big stone wheel. After these are crushed, they are put into a press, and the oil trickles into large vats beneath.

I have been to Venice—that wonderland, where all the roads are waterways, and, instead of riding in carriages, everyone goes about in gondolas. There are no less than 150 of these water streets, and the houses are built on piles and rise directly from the water. In front of the houses are gaily painted posts, to which the gondolas can anchor for the people to get in and out. These gondolas are long flat-bottomed boats, and are always painted black. Hundreds of these are always passing along the water streets, for all the tradesmen deliver their goods by gondolas, just the same as the people have to go to church or the theatre in them. The first time I ever went in one of these gondolas, Maria whispered in my ear: "Now, Filomena, watch our gondolier." And so, you may be sure, I did. He stood up, and instead of using the oar in the usual way, he pushed out into the water instead of pulling. All the strokes are made on one side only, and the oar is hardly ever lifted out of the water. The Grand Canal is a marvellous sight, both by night and day, for it is two miles long and always crowded with gondolas; while the view from the Piazza, with the great dome of St. Mark's, is the finest

Peeps at the World's Dolls

in Europe. Beside myself, Maria has another doll whose name is Isabelle, and who was given her by an aunt. She is very charming indeed, and comes from one of the coast villages where she used to be a fisher-girl. She wears a pair of ear-rings, and a white blouse that is just gathered in at the neck to a narrow band. The sleeves come right down to the wrist and are very full, ending in a frill. Over this she wears a corselet of black velvet, drawn together with scarlet laces, while her skirt has a couple of scarlet bands at the bottom. The lovely embroidery on her apron is gold and blue and green and pink and orange. Her stockings are white, while her boots are of untanned leather. On her head she wears a gaily coloured square scarf which is crimson and green and orange.

We are three very happy people, and I love Isabelle almost as much as I do Maria, for we always go everywhere together, and share all the pleasures that we can.

CHAPTER VIII

MARIA THERESA, OF HUNGARY

MARIA THERESA, that is my little owner's name, and she is one of the happiest, healthiest, round-cheeked, bright-eyed girls in all the world. My

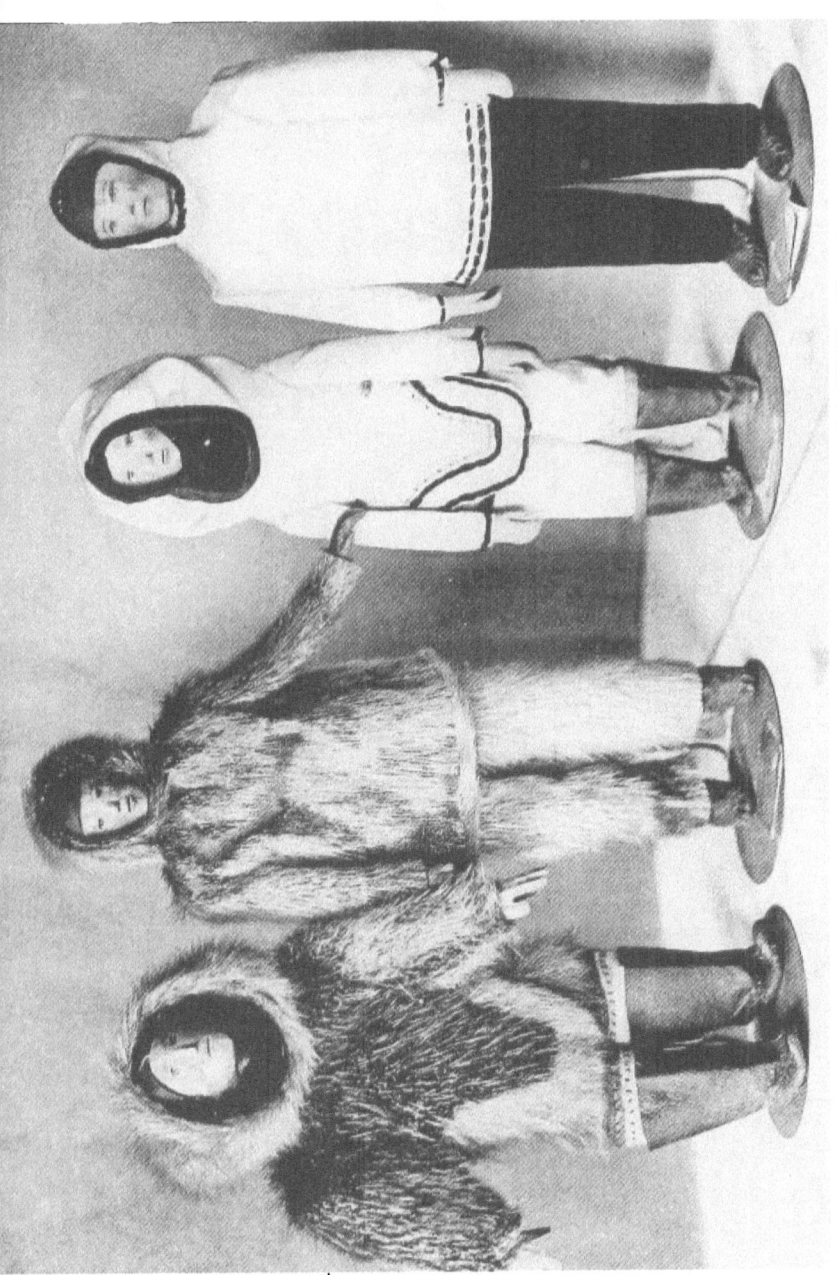

DOLLS FROM LAPLAND IN THE TYPICAL WINTER AND SUMMER DRESS. Page 20.

Maria Theresa, of Hungary

own name is Panna, and we belong to the peasant class of people, and I think that I am one of the best-loved dolly girls in the whole of our great country. I wish you could see our cottage home, where we both live so joyfully together.

Quite a lot of us cannot read nor write, but Maria Theresa can just manage to scribble her name in a very shaky way, and she can slowly spell out words in big books; so that when she grows up she will be considered quite clever and advanced. But I was telling you about our cottage home. Every cottage in our country is built on the side of a small garden or court, that is separated from the roadway by a line of fencing, and most of the windows are placed so that they look on to the road, so that when it is a wet day, or we want to be amused, we can see everyone who happens to pass by on their journeys to the town. Under the windows runs a long bench which is called a " sychordo " (which means " bearer of words "), and it is on this that people sit and gossip, sometimes for hours together. Maria Theresa often sits here, with me cuddled close up against her warm little body, and sings to me so that her musical crooning voice and the warmth soon send me fast asleep, and then I wake up—perhaps long hours afterwards—and find that she has laid me down and gone indoors to have her dinner.

The roof of our house is thatched with straw

Peeps at the World's Dolls

or reeds, and this roof projects into very broad eaves over a brick terrace that runs all round the house. This is done because of the wet time that comes in the winter season, so that we can walk in the dry without stepping into the mud that lies everywhere when the weather is bad. Some of the larger houses are built in two parts, on either side of the garden, instead of one; and, where this is so the two portions are connected by a lofty arch gateway.

Always the house is whitewashed, and generally decorated here and there with bright colours, for we are very fond of a gay appearance in everything.

And this brings me to myself and the wonderful clothes that Maria Theresa herself has made for me. I said that we were a peasant family, and so, of course, I am garbed in the national dress, for we are the only class that still continues in the old ways. Indeed, if you looked at me you would almost see Maria Theresa, for she has copied every detail of her own dress so exactly that, except that she is dark and I am fair, there is hardly any difference in us.

First of all, I wear a cap, and it is one of the prettiest caps imaginable. It is woven by hand of cotton, and is white or cream in colour. But the point about it is the wonderful embroidery that Maria Theresa has stitched into it in red and scarlet silk. This may sound funny to you, but when

HUNGARIAN DOLLS. Page 24

Maria Theresa, of Hungary

it is worked and all filled in between with violet and green, you would be charmed with the appearance, for none of the original white cotton, of which the cap is made, shows at all. My skirt and blouse are both of similar white cotton, worked all over with a black and red spot pattern, done in cross stitch. Over my blouse I wear a sleeveless plain coat of dark blue, lined with red silk and edged with a border of white pinked cloth. Down the front of this coat are two rows of tiny silver buttons, so that you can see I am very smart indeed. But this is not all, for I wear a little cotton apron and a sash of woven wool, in the brightest mixture of colours you can imagine. To complete me (and I should have felt sad indeed without this) I have a long necklace of black and red beads that Maria Theresa threaded for me one winter for a Christmas gift.

Sometimes we have very gay times indeed, for we are a light-hearted people and one of our chief joys is dancing. When the shepherds come into the village is the best time, for they never seem to get tired of playing the "tilinka," and everyone dances the whole evening and far into the night. Maria Theresa is as fond of this as anyone, and, rather than miss a dance, takes me by my hands for her partner, until everyone exclaims: "Just look at Maria Theresa and Panna! What a girl she is!"

Peeps at the World's Dolls

CHAPTER IX
THE PRECIOUS CHILD OF KOREA

"Precious child!" you exclaim. Yes, I should think that I am one of the most precious children in the world, for more than a hundred of my mother's neighbours took an oath, at the time when I came to live in her home, to do everything that they could to protect and care for me.

Of course, I am only a dolly of that little-known land Korea, but you can see that I am a very beautifully made one, and on the day that I first came to my dear little mistress, Kwang-chu, she insisted on the usual national custom being carried out in my honour.

All the children in our village were asked to come to my birthday, and it is here that the strange story begins, a story that is true of every little boy and girl that lives in that far-off country. When a new little baby is born, it is a time of the greatest rejoicing, and all the neighbours come swarming in, each one carrying a piece of stuff (usually silk) in one of the brightest colours they can find, as a present for the new child. The gift of this piece of silk is a symbol, and means that everyone who makes such a gift pledges himself or herself to do everything he or she can to

The Precious Child of Korea

guard and look after the little stranger; so that, you see, the Korean children are always well looked after, if they happen to stray away and be beyond their parents' control.

It was a very wonderful idea of Kwang-chu to invite all the other little girls and boys to my first birthday, so that each one should bring me a piece of silk for my "precious child jacket," so that if any of them ever found me in danger, or lost, I should at once be brought back to her—the best place on earth.

After the party was over and all the boys and girls had gone home again, Kwang-chu gathered together all the little pieces of stuff and began to stitch and sew them together into a coat with loose sleeves, so that it slipped on and off easily without bending my arms back too far. It took her a long time, you may be sure, because, you see the pieces were many different shapes and sizes, and they had to be fitted together so as to make the best use of the material. I was proud the first time she put my jacket on me and I saw all the wonderful bright colours looking so cheerful. I expect that I shall wear my "precious" jacket for as long as ever I am a dolly, but the live children in Korea, both boys and girls, only wear them until they are three and a half years old, when the boys are put into boys' clothing and the girls into girls'. Until that time they both wear very long

Peeps at the World's Dolls

skirts, so long that they completely hide the long trousers that come right down to the ankles. And then, my shoes! I must tell you about those. The soles are made of plaited fibre and the uppers of openwork twisted string. They are very "comfy" to wear, because they bend every time my foot does, and I should not like the hard boots and shoes that English dolls have to wear.

Yes, altogether my land, Korea, is a very happy one to live in. Kwang-chu treasures me as the light of her eyes, I have a gorgeous "precious child jacket" that would make many other real live Koreans very envious, and over a hundred friends are pledged to care for me, and that is more than most people could say.

By the way, I want you to take one more look at my picture and see how well Kwang-chu has made my coat. Every single piece stitched together by her own chubby hands. It is not an uncommon matter at all nowadays for cloth, all woven in one piece and dyed in different colours, to be sold in the markets to make the "precious child jackets," but mine is one of the real old-fashioned kind, with all the pieces sewn together by my mistress, and I am very proud of it and of her too.

Some Strange Dolls

CHAPTER X

SOME STRANGE DOLLS

I WONDER what you would say if you could see some of the strange dolls with which the young girls play in the smaller and more out-of-the-way parts of the world, and the quaint and curious things that are used to make them. If you lived in Bermuda, for instance, it is quite likely that you would love a doll made from banana pith. Made from banana pith ? Yes, banana pith, and with nuts for heads, and the funniest little hats and bonnets, also plaited from pith, stuck on these nut heads. Perhaps one of the funniest dolls of all are those with which the negro girls of the Gold Coast play. Anything less like our idea of a doll it would be difficult to imagine, for it has no body nor head nor arms, but is formed from a perfectly flat piece of wood which is shaped rather like a spade, except that the handle, too, is flat. The wood from which it is cut is usually light in colour, and a certain amount of ornamentation in criss-cross is done on one side with a brownish pigment. Nothing less like the human figure could possibly be imagined, and yet that is their idea of dolly—the only dolly they have ever known—and she is loved and played with just in

Peeps at the World's Dolls

the same way that the grown-up people in those lands worship an idol as their god.

Sometime, when you are in London, try and persuade someone to take you to the British Museum, where they have some very old and curious dolls on exhibition. Those of ancient Egypt are extremely curious and most ingeniously made. The arms and legs are jointed and move by means of strings, so that the dolls could be made to dance; while examples have been unearthed that had hair made of mud beads, and furnished with a squeaking arrangement, worked by means of bellows, which are very like those of the cheaper Japanese dolls that are imported into England to-day. Then, too, you can see a wonderful bronze woman doll, carrying a pot upon her head, having been to the well to draw water, and another of flat painted wood with strings of beads for hair. Think of the wonder of it! Thousands and thousands of years ago lived little girls, taught differently, clothed differently, dwelling in different lands, yet they had their crude dollies to carry and talk to, just the same as we have.

Among the tombs of the earlier Christians it is not an uncommon matter for explorers to find the mummified bodies of small girls, and, with them, their quaint little dollies. Many quaint old dolls are rapidly dying out, and among these I should

Some Strange Dolls

like to tell you about our own Harvest Doll. This is a real British dolly, though it is now getting very rare indeed. Down in the West country, when the harvest is all reaped, the least ears of corn gathered from the field are put aside and taken home to the house. Then someone binds this up into the effigy of a doll. The head is composed of a tuft of the ears of corn, and round the neck is a bow of brightly coloured ribbon. For arms, two tufts of the stalk stick out, and round these the ribbon passes, finally hanging down in a tab at the front. The body is very long and consists of plaited stems bound together with cotton or thread. This marvellous dolly is hung in the farmer's house with great ceremony until the next harvest is completed, and then a new one is made and the old one solemnly burned.

Another very strange doll is that which one sometimes sees made in Yorkshire—the Bread Doll. This is made exactly like a real baby, but from the ordinary bread dough. Its arms and legs are made as shapely as possible, with the fingers or toes marked out by a knife. There is an incision made to represent the open mouth, with a small pointed dab of dough for the nose, while a couple of currants are pressed in for small black eyes. This dolly is baked very lightly, so that it shall not be too dark brown, and, when complete, is dressed in a set of white infant's robes,

Peeps at the World's Dolls

and I can tell you that it makes one of the most curious-looking dollies in the world.

Another doll is that made from ordinary bun-dough. She, as a rule, does not live long, for most people eat her very soon after she leaves the baker's oven, because she is full of currants and candied peel, and tastes very good indeed at tea-time, after the bread-and-butter is done with. She is not so pretty to look at as the bread doll, and is always much more roughly made. But still, she has a head, a body, two short arms, and long, thick legs. I have never seen her dress at all, but she has currants for eyes and a row of currants down the front to represent the buttons of her blouse.

All dolls are not beautiful by any means, and I am sure that you would agree with this if you could see one that came from Zanzibar. This is a very remarkable-looking creature indeed, though it boasts the beauty of "real hair." This is native hair, very black, coarse, and "frizzy," so much so that it is just like a bundle of horsehair. The face and body are formed of plaited palm-leaves, the eyes and nose and mouth being represented by red ribbons stitched through the palm. It wears enormous paper earrings, just the same as those worn by the grown-up girls in this strange island, while both the arms and ankles are circled by beads, just in the same way as are those of the

A KOREAN DOLL.

Some Strange Dolls

babies. The arms are long, so are the legs, and consist of a series of nuts threaded together.

Another most unusual doll superstition, that at one time was very common in Belgium, was the doll that was given to the baby children (girls and boys) when they were cutting their first teeth. In England we generally give them something hard, such as a bone ring, etc., to bite and so help their teeth to come through the tender gums, but in Belgium they used to make a special dolly. This was dressed in white clothes, and pinned to the dress with a safety-pin was—a tooth. A strange idea, truly, that by playing with a doll, of which a tooth was one of the ornaments, the live baby should grow its teeth more easily.

Families of dolls, too, are by no means uncommon in some of the lands over the sea, a very typical set of these being Indian. They have one of these sets in the South Kensington Museum. Little gaily painted figures on wooden stands, each one of which represents some different trade or station in life. The party consists of seven figures, and includes a snake charmer with a cobra coiled in front of him; a flour grinder, with his primitive mill; a cotton winder, with her spool and thread; a toddy climber, who swarms the tree and gathers the fruit from which this drink is brewed; an old woman with very white hair; an

Peeps at the World's Dolls

old man, with his staff to support him; and a policeman dressed in his white uniform and distinctive turban.

In every Chinaman's house, too, you would find a most curious " set," or family, of dolls. They are dressed in most gorgeous colours, and represent different gods or virtues, and no home is complete without them.

And now that we have talked of all these strange dolls, the list is not anything like complete. We might go on to the wonderful doll made by the Witch Doctors in the Congo, dolls that are supposed to protect from drowning when the men go fishing, dolls that are supposed to guard against headache, dolls that are supposed to look after a man's soul, and prevent it being stolen while he is asleep, etc.; but I must only tell you of one more, and that is made in Korea from straw. This is a most grotesque-looking creature that, however, does bear some kind of likeness to a human being. The workmanship is really good, and the dolls are most cleverly fashioned. The body is entirely of stuffed straw, with a large round head, upon which the eyes, nose, and mouth are drawn. The arms and legs are in two parts, so as to represent the elbow and knee joints, although they do not bend, while each foot and hand ends in five long toes, or fingers, made in plaited straw. Offerings are made to these queer dollies, under the idea that

La Belle Française

they will bring good luck, and it is no uncommon matter to see them with these offerings of coins stuck between the straw of which their arms are made.

CHAPTER XI

LA BELLE FRANÇAISE

AH, but yes! I do want to tell you all about myself, and my country, and my dear Ninette, who loves me so much.

Perhaps it is that I do—how do you call it?—" speak "—yes, yes, that is it!—" speak " your language in the funny way, and you will laugh at my English, but that matters not. We do understand each other, there is *le bon camaraderie*, and if you speak the French to me—well, I laugh also. I have been in your wonderful land and seen your London, and I like it, but La Belle France, that, to me, is better. For I love my land; I love my Paris; I love my Nice and Toulouse, with its wonderful churches; and I love Ninette.

For myself, I am a Parisian, one of the most accomplished and exquisite dolls in all the world; but now I live in Nice, the Land of Flowers, where the gay sun is always smiling and we all smile too.

For Ninette, nothing is too good. Alphonse, the old gardener; Marguerite, her nurse; Jeanette —how we all do love her, and how she does love us in return. Her kiss is the sweetest thing in life, and, though I am only her dolly, when those soft lips caress my cheek and the same lips whisper in my ear, something inside me stirs and leaps in a way that would surprise you humans. My hair is fair, with a rare gleaming gold in it, for, of course, it is "real" and once grew on the little head of a southern peasant girl before it adorned my own head.

And my dresses! Of course, I have numberless Parisian dresses and hats, so that I am fit to appear upon any and every occasion—*une bien élevée*, as the aristocratic French girl is called. All of these beautiful clothes were packed into a—how do you say it?—case?—no, a little trunk. Ah, my little trunk! It is so chic, and every one of my so lovely dresses does just pack in, so that nothing is spoiled. Yes, it is very good and quite charming. With this are my shoes and gloves—again, good. Dainty little shoes, and slippers to match my dress or frock. My tailor-made gown for outdoors, my morning gown that I wear in the house until after *déjeuner*, my glorious evening dresses! Never, never, never would you find so well equipped a dolly as I am outside La Belle France. My lingerie, my brush, and toilet requisites—all are perfect. And what a chattering there is, and how we all laugh together, while Ninette is changing my clothes and making me look so pretty

FRENCH FISHERFOLK DOLLS. Page 40.

La Belle Française

to go on the Boulevard with her! Yes, she is the most "spoiled" little girl in Europe, but, ah! how sweet and attractive and vivacious! From early morning, when she has finished her *café au lait*, until she goes to sleep again, life is just one long song, and it is to me just so good to be with her when the night has come as it is while the light is with us. Every night she unrobes me and puts me to sleep close beside her, and I shut the eyes—ah, yes!—just the same as she does do. In the winter-time, many and many people from your country do come to stay in Nice with us, and, indeed, we are then the very cosmopolitan country; for, to escape the fogs and the dulness of other colder and less sunny lands, many people of all nationalities do come. And so we are always gay and merry with the charming people, and always the flowers.

Often when we are out, Ninette and I, we meet the English girls with their dolls, and one day last year I did see an American girl with her New York doll, that walked by her side just like a live thing. It is possible that you have heard of this, but to me it was new, and I did stare. For this dolly walked—yes, walked!—exactly the same as her proud young mistress did. I would that I could have talked with them; but no! the English of Ninette was not good, for she is a very little girl, and the French with her has to be first.

Peeps at the World's Dolls

One day she will it speak as I can write it, and then she will perhaps see London and New York and the other wonderful cities of the earth—yes, it is possible.

And now let me take up the tale and tell you something about the wonderful French fisher dolls that are shown in the picture. These are real French dolls, dressed by the coast peasants just in the ordinary everyday clothes in which they work and live. The old lady in the centre is a typical fishwife in her holiday dress, with lace apron and handsomely embroidered shawl and lace cap. On the left is her daughter, with striped skirt and knitted cardigan, carrying a basket of fish and one of the nets. Notice that she is barefooted and wears no stockings, because of the sea in which she so often wades to bring the catch ashore when the menfolk return. On the right hand is her son, a hefty youth with his wooden-soled sea-clogs, and oilskins rolled up in his hand. Except that he has slipped out of his oilskins, he is just as he went to sea and stepped ashore. Over one shoulder is a coil of rope, on the other his trawl with the cork "bobbers," as the English fisherman calls them, that float on the surface and show the position of the net in the sea. Everything is complete, just as you see the fishermen day after day in Brittany, with their stockinette

La Belle Française

caps, which at one time are worn with the bag flopping loose, as shown in the photo, and at others rolled over so that they fit closely down upon the head. Do you notice the little clay pipe that is grasped in his right hand, and, above all, the old retriever dog? This dog is quite as much a sailor as his master, and never fails to go to sea on every trip that his master takes. Indeed, he would rush about the quay whining most pitifully if, by chance, he were left behind.

It is a hard life for both the boys and the girls who have to earn their living in that way, and the mother, too, works almost equally hard in her little shop where the fish is sold.

CHAPTER XII
SOUTH AFRICA

A LITTLE lump of clay, beaten and pounded until it became quite plastic: that is how Mam-baumi started life as a doll. For among the Kaffirs of South Africa, about whom I am now going to tell you, the parents never give their children toys to play with, but each child makes his own.

As I was saying, Mam-baumi started life just as a lump of clay, beaten and pounded until it was quite soft, and so could be twisted and moulded

Peeps at the World's Dolls

into any shape that was desired. Until this point there was quite a doubt as to whether she would be a doll or an animal, such as a sheep, ox, or dog, but the litle Kaffir girl—such a funny little dark-skinned girl—decided that it was to be a doll, and that her name was to be Mam-baumi. All her brothers and sisters sat round, watching to see what form the clay was to take. Presently, as the busy fingers worked, the clay began to take a shape, and they saw that it was to be the funniest little clay doll, very short and stumpy, but with arms, legs, and head all complete. When these strange dolls are finished, they are left in the hot sunlight for several days to bake and harden, and are then ready to be played with. And what games they do have, too, faithfully copying, in every detail, different phases of their own and the grown-ups' daily life.

A very popular game with the children is weddings, and for this quite a number of dolls, oxen, etc., are needed. One boy doll is made, and a number of girls and a suitable number of oxen, so that each girl may bring her dowry to her husband. But before the wedding can take place a house or kraal must be built for the married folks to live in. This is the work of the boys, and a wonderfully skilful job they make of it. Sticks and mud are used in its building, and it is an exact copy of their own dwellings.

South Africa

This house is round in shape, and several huts are generally set down together, circled round by a hedge of bushes. The sticks are set up and held together with daub and mud that very quickly dries in the hot sunshine. As a means of entrance, there is a low doorway which can be closed at night by means of a hurdle, but this is the only opening of any kind that there is, as no windows or chimneys are thought to be necessary.

At the middle of the hut a small depression is formed in the beaten floor, with a ring of earth round it, which serves as a fireplace, and where, in the live people's huts, a fire is always burning, night and day, The air inside is simply suffocating, for, remember, that there are neither windows nor chimney, so that all the smoke from the fire is always floating about inside, and slowly making its way out through the chinks and crevices—the best way it can. The boys build this doll's house extremely neatly, and when the walls, etc., are complete, thatching the roof is left to the girls. Even yet they are not ready to play weddings, for there is the furniture, etc., to be provided, and a number of clay pots, jars, etc., are formed and baked in the sun; then there are the oxen, wives, etc. Most of the remaining furniture consists of a few baskets, some sleeping mats, and wooden pillows. Then the clothes must be provided.

Peeps at the World's Dolls

The Kaffirs have a great love for European clothing, and will wear the most extraordinary combination of garments that ever you saw. The native girls and women almost all wear leather petticoats, that are made very soft by fraying, and, sometimes, tiny ones of these are made for the dolls, in imitation of their little owners. And then the great game of wedding begins, and what shouts of joy and laughter accompany it—for the Kaffirs are the merriest little children in all the world—until, finally, the brides are brought home in triumph to the dolls' house, that has been built with such pains and care.

Sometimes the game is varied and takes the form of beer-drinking; for the children will imitate, in their play, everything that they see the grown-ups do, and everything can be turned into a doll game by the exercise of a little imagination.

Sometimes the girls make a very curious doll from the Indian corn stalks. This dolly is made of the corn-cob, then all the grains are stripped off and the cob dressed in a piece of blanket. Two beads are used to form the eyes, and pieces of wool are ravelled out from the blanket, so as to make the hair which is stuck on the top. No Kaffir girl is allowed to take her doll to bed with her, so that all the " cuddly " times take place during the day, but she loves her funny little

NORWEGIAN PEASANT DOLL. Page 48.
Representing a peasant girl in holiday dress.

Harald, the Norwegian

clay or corn-cob dolly just as much as you would love the most splendid wax or porcelain doll from London or Paris.

CHAPTER XIII

HARALD, THE NORWEGIAN

HARALD? Yes! That is my name, and I am one of the most curiously dressed of all Norwegian dollies, for, although I am very like an English doll with very fair hair and very blue eyes, my clothes are quite special. My little mistress has two of us. I am from Saetersdal, dressed in the old-time costume, and Greta comes from Hardanger; and while my clothes are the most curious, yet hers are certainly the most picturesque, so that my mistress loves us both, and everyone who sees us looks with equal interest.

Let me tell you about myself first. I am a boy doll and so, you see, I wear an enormous pair of "buxer," or trousers, that come right up to my neck both back and front, and which are kept in place by shoulder-straps. In front I wear a breast-plate, ornamented with embroidery in green cloth, and rows of silver buttons. At my ankles are more pieces of embroidery on green cloth, though these are not so grand as the ones at the breast. On the back of the trousers is an immense leather patch, while the legs are dark brown vadmel. These are my working clothes, but for Sundays and festive occasions I have a jacket and pair of white sleeves with which I wear a white shirt, fastened at the neck with very handsome silver studs. The girl dolls of my country wear very short skirts, scarcely reaching to the knees, and at the waist a leather belt with ornamental silver buttons. The bodice is white and very full, fastened at the neck and wrists with handsome silver studs. These studs are quite one of the features of the women's and girls' dress, and far more elaborate than those of the men. Below the skirt are long woollen stockings, almost invariably dark in colour, and held in place below the knees by silver garters. The shoes are very curiously turned up at the toes, while the head is covered by a scarf so that hardly any of the hair shows at all.

And now let me tell you about Greta, who comes from Hardanger. She is dressed in a white skirt and very full sleeves, over which she wears a red embroidered bodice and a short, full, black skirt with red braid round the hem. I must tell you about a strange hat that the older women wear in Hardanger, and which Greta declares she has often seen when she was living there. This is called the "regnhat," and if you divide the word into

Harald, the Norwegian

two syllables and say it slowly, you will not be long in understanding what it means—"rain hat," and a very suitable name too, for it is quite as good as any umbrella. The brim of this unusual hat is made of tarred felt and completely covers the shoulders, so that when heavy rain comes the wearer is quite safely protected. Well, that is how we look in our special dresses, though my little mistress herself is not so very different from the English girls and wears very much the same clothes.

We, in common with many other of the Continental nations, are very fond of dancing, and quite among the curiosities in this way is the dance called the " halling." Last year, when we were in the country (for we all of us leave the cities and go into the country when the summer comes), I saw them dance this one evening, at an old wooden farmhouse where we were staying for a week. First of all, the dancer squatted on the floor, and then hopped sideways, in time with the music of a violin. This was followed by swaying to and fro as though he were going to leap, then the side hopping was resumed as before, faster and faster, faster and faster, until quite suddenly he threw his head backwards and with a great leap kicked the beam of the ceiling. How we all did laugh and shout, and my young mistress held me up by two arms, and made me clap my hands together

Peeps at the World's Dolls

in applause. I did enjoy the wonderful life at this farm, and saw many things that looked very strange in the customs and many beautiful sights of the countryside. Most of the dwelling-houses are built of timber and are placed quite close together because of the cold weather in the winter, when it would be impossible for the people to go out far distances.

Then we have quantities of fruits; the blaaboer, which you know as bilberry, grows everywhere, and wild raspberries are nearly as abundant, and my little mistress had a great time gathering and eating both of these.

In the cottages the peasant girls always have wooden dolls; not a bit like I am, with my lovely fair hair and blue eyes, but dolls that their fathers cut out for them from blocks of wood, which they bring in from the forest. Quite wonderful dolls complete with beautifully modelled limbs and faces, for which their mothers make the most lovely clothes, just like their own, and upon which they spend hours and hours—stitch! stitch! stitch!—to complete the lovely embroidery with which the plainest piece of material is trimmed.

Chandi and Kali

CHAPTER XIV

CHANDI AND KALI

LOOK well at these two strange figures, Chandi, the mother, accompanied by Kali, her own little baby. Did you ever see two more remarkable dolls ? They have a very strange history that I think you would like to hear, and are exactly typical of the dolls with which the girl children in the great country of India play. It was scorchingly hot although it was only seven o'clock in the morning, but nothing like so hot as it would be later in the day, when all the Europeans have to remain indoors because of the sun. The mother of the little girl to whom the dolly belonged was little more than a child herself, and, of course, lived in the zenana, or women's part of the house, where there are swarms of children as well as other women. She herself did not do much for her little girl, because she had an ayah who nursed and tended her.

This ayah moved very quietly, because she wore no shoes when in the house. That would be considered the most disrespectful thing she could do; although, when in the street, she wore loose goat hide slippers without heels. Her dress was of

Peeps at the World's Dolls

woven cotton, very soft in texture, and over the skirt she wore a tunic that hung to a depth of three to four inches below the waist-line. This tunic buttons in the front with three sets of buttons. Round her feet she had metal anklets which clanked together as she walked. Her hair was parted down the middle, drawn back tightly behind the ears, and fastened at the back into a tight knob without any hairpins.

This ayah had but one thing to do, and that was to look after the little dark-skinned baby. As the baby lay in the ayah's arms, she laughed and crooned just as all the other little baby girls do when they are quite small, and then she slept and slept for long hours together. And it was while she slept that the ayah made the funny looking doll for her to play with, that you see in the photograph. The arms, body, and legs are made of the finest white cotton material, while the head is of some kind of skin, and all are stuffed quite firm and solid with odd rags. The faces are drawn on the skin, and a tiny nose stuck upon the face, so that quite a wonderful expression is given to this mother dolly. Then the baby was made in the same way, only, of course, on a much smaller scale. Tiny bead bangles were placed round the arms of both mother and baby, and then they were both ready to be dressed. All

Chandi and Kali

Hindoos love bright colours, and especially the babies; therefore very brilliant colouring was chosen for the dress. The long skirt was vivid mauve purple, with bands of tinsel silver between the colour, and a broad band of similar silver tinsel round the bottom. The curious cloak shawl was made of the same material, as was the headdress, and in both cases the same band of silver ran round the edge.

Well, one day, when the dark-skinned baby grew older, she was playing in the zenana with Chandi, when a most wonderful thing happened that threw everyone into a flutter, for they were visited by a white missionary lady who could speak Hindustani. For days after she had gone the women and children talked of her, and wondered how soon she would come again. Did she come again? Oh, yes, and before very long too. It was a very great privilege for her, and before a month had passed she was back again, chatting as brightly as ever. And what do you think she brought with her? Ah, indeed you would never guess. A real English dolly, that she herself had dressed with English clothes, and that she put into the hands of the little Hindoo girl. Everyone was almost wild with excitement, and the girl-women, who lived in the zenana, were nearly as crazy about it as the child herself. Indeed, I think more so; for, you see, they were

Peeps at the World's Dolls

but little more than children too. How they did stare, and how they examined every article of this wonder-doll's dress! They crowded round and laughed and laughed, while each one examined her in turn. At last the missionary lady took her and replaced her in the little girl's arms, and, in return, asked if she might have Chandi and Kali to send to a little girl in her own far-off England. At first everybody said "No," and the ayah offered to make another new and very clean one in their place. But no! nothing would do but Chandi and Kali. She wanted a real Hindoo doll, that a Hindoo girl had played with. And so, at last, she got her way, and she took Chandi and Kali from the dark little hand and placed the lovely English doll in its place, and the pair, Chandi and Kali, set out upon the great journey to England, where they arrived safely, and are looked upon as two of the most wonderful dolls in all the neighbourhood where they live. A pair of real Hindoo dolls, taken from the dark hand of a real Hindoo girl.

AN INDIAN NATIVE DOLL REPRESENTING MOTHER AND HER CHILD (CHANDI AND KALI). Page 49.

Switzerland

CHAPTER XV

SWITZERLAND

HURRAH! Hurrah! At last the great day has come and everyone is delighted—everyone except Gretel, who feels extremely sad, because Christian, her beloved brother, is going away to the pastures with the men and the cattle, and she will not see him again for weeks to come. She just sits still on her stool beside the door, with her dolly on her lap, watching all the preparations with one big ache in her heart, because few people were ever closer or loved each other more than Christian and Gretel.

It is one of the great events of the year in the Alpine villages, when the flocks and herds are taken to summer pastures. The animals that lead the herds are gaily decked with flowers and bells, and the boys, who accompany them with the men, all sing for joy. Christian, of course, is just as excited as anyone else; indeed, I think more so, for, you see, this was the first time that he had been old enough to go.

But you may be sure he had not forgotten Gretel, and it was the one dark spot in the bright day that she looked so sorrowful at parting from

Peeps at the World's Dolls

him. Just before they went, he rushed over to her, and flung his arms round her neck and gave her two kisses on each cheek, and then shyly produced the wonderful present which he had procured so secretly for her. I do not suppose you will have much difficulty in guessing what it was—a superb doll.

Not at all the ordinary kind of doll, but a splendid town shop doll, with the most glorious blue eyes, fair hair, and pink cheeks. Even if she had not been half as beautiful, the love that prompted such a generous thought would have filled Gretel's eyes with happy tears, and it certainly did much to ease the pain of parting. Kindly thoughts do so much in this world, and Christian was overjoyed at Gretel's happiness and pleasure, while he knew that she would enjoy the busy times of dressing the wonderful doll and surprising him with its handsome clothes when he came back again. For, do not make any mistake upon that point, the girls have to work in Switzerland quite as hard and early as the boys do. They can all assist when the haytime comes, and Gretel was even then learning to make butter. Christian was going this year with the cows because it was his first time, but as he grew older he would set off with the sheep and goats to the higher lands, where the grazing is merely in patches amid the snow. These grazing grounds are reached by

Switzerland

steep, narrow paths, and such work is very good training for becoming an Alpine guide, which was Christian's great ambition. In the winter all the family is at home together, and much of the life has to be lived indoors, because of the snow, although the sun shines brightly, sometimes for weeks together. Life is very good then, and in the weeks that followed, when Gretel was often thinking about Christian, away with the herds in the pastures, she often looked forward to the time when the short summer would be over, and her beloved brother would be with her again. The Swiss are extremely handy and clever workmen, and no doubt you have seen some of the lovely carving that they do so exquisitely. This is not only done in wood, but in ivory too, and some very wonderful flowers are carved in the latter. Christian had a great idea in his head all the summer, and when he came home again, and saw the care that Gretel had taken in dressing the doll that he left with her, he was so pleased that he at once set about the work which he had in his mind. One day, when he came in from feeding the cattle, he brought with him several pieces of wood sawn up into planks. Gretel was filled with curiosity as to what he could be going to do, but he only laughed, and told her that one day she would know a lot more about it than she did now. But he was only teasing, and at last he told her what was in his mind. This was nothing less than building a wonderful home for the dolls—a dolls' house which should be worthy of the great lady that was to occupy it.

Day by day the building grew, until the roof was on, the stairs were in, the doors were cut between the rooms, and a perfect model of a Swiss home was waiting to be occupied.

And how happy both were in the doing: Gretel in her brother's love, and Christian in her pleasure! Even when the dolls' house was completed, this was by no means the end, for then the furniture had to be made. Chairs and tables and wonderful wooden beds all followed in succession, until Gretel was the owner of the best dolls and the best dollies' house in all that part of Switzerland.

CHAPTER XVI

DOLORES, OF SUNNY SPAIN

Sunny Spain! What a delightful impression of the wonderful land where oranges grow out of doors and the sun seems to be shining through the greater part of the year. My own name is Dolores, and I live with my little owner, Isabel, in Cadiz, one of the chief cities in all that sunny land. We have one of the most splendid harbours in the world, and our city is extremely old, for it was founded at least

Dolores, of Sunny Spain

three thousand years ago. I wish you could see Isabel, for she is a typical Spanish girl, with pleasing and gracious ways and delightful manners; although, like the rest of us, she is very passionate and easily roused. But as we can hate well, so we can love deeply, and I am devoted to Isabel, and never happy when she is far away from me. She has an olive complexion, dark eyes, and masses of curly black hair that looks simply wonderful in the sunlight. And it is a curious thing that, wherever you go in Spain, and however many little girls you see with their dolls, you will hardly ever see one with fair hair or blue yes, but always the Spanish dark ones. I do not go out in a perambulator like the English dolly does; Isabel always carries me in her arms, and I always feel very proud of the easy, graceful way in which she walks as we go along the street. As a nation we are very fond of bright colours, and so you may be sure that I have no lack of brilliant clothes to wear. My usual dress is that worn on fête days by a young lady. My skirt has a frilled hem and is just above my ankles in length. My stockings are white and my shoes black, and over my skirt I wear an apron with blue and white stripes. Quite the most brilliant thing about my clothes is my shawl, which is of silk, very often orange in colour, with red and green flowers, and always with a broad black fringe running all round the edge.

Peeps at the World's Dolls

This is worn cornerways so as to show the bare throat, round which there are two or three rows of beads.

When I am not wearing my shawl and apron, I have a black lace scarf with which to drape my hair, and this is called a mantilla. My hair is a great point with me, and is dressed right on the top of my head, with a very tall comb stuck in behind, but so that it shows from the front. Most of the folks that you would meet in the streets are not, of course, dressed like this, but just in the ordinary way. Travelling in my land is a very slow business indeed, and in many places it is only possible by carts drawn by oxen. A great deal of shouting seems to be necessary to get these carts along, and the first time Isabel took me into the country with her, I was greatly puzzled by all the noise and excitement. Another point, too, that struck me as very curious was the wheels with which the bullock carts are fitted. They are of the most primitive form and only cut from a single round of wood. I did not like my ride at all, I can assure you, and I was very glad when we got to my mistress's uncle's house and the jolting ceased. For we had bumped for hours over the worst possible road, and I heartily wished that I was back in Cadiz again, although it is nice to see your own land and some of the quaint customs that still remain.

Samoa

CHAPTER XVII

SAMOA

Swish! A great wave is just curling over its crest ere it breaks and falls. A shriek—then several more. Crash! The wave has broken, and comes swirling up the beach as it bubbles and boils in masses of white froth. Yell after yell of laughter, as a number of little brown figures scramble to their feet and grab at their small boards ere the receding wave sucks them back into the sea again. That is the scene I am watching as I sit with my back against a rock, high and dry above the reach of the incoming tide.

For I am a little Samoan dolly, and a lot of boys and girls from our village are playing at their favourite game of surf-riding. Every one of them is a wonderful swimmer, and this is one of the favourite games. My owner is that lovely bright-eyed girl who has just plunged into the sea again with her board, and her name is Kopiolani. Let us watch. There she goes, making her way through the water as easily as if she were walking on dry land, with her little board held in front of her in one hand. Now—see how she is waiting there, in the rough sea, for a big wave to

Peeps at the World's Dolls

come along. Ah, here it is! Yes, it has caught her up and is racing her towards the shore at a great rate. Crash! how it thundered down! And there is Kopiolani, high and dry upon the sand, laughing as she wipes the water from her face and brushes back her drenching hair. Yes, she has had enough of it now, and is coming towards the rock where she left me before entering the sea.

Though I am far from beautiful, as you would consider beauty—being only cut from a block of wood and quite roughly painted to represent a human face—yet I appear to Kopiolani as a very lovable doll indeed, and she makes her way straight back to my resting-place. Up she gathers me in her arms, and, with a whole crowd of other girls who have been surf-riding, we set out to search the rock pools, etc., that are still uncovered by the incoming tide. And what a wonderland this all is, for the whole shore is covered with shells and treasures, as well as small crabs and pieces of coral and seaweed. Kopiolani is very keen on the shells, for she is very busily collecting enough of one particular kind to make a necklace for me. She herself always wears one, and has been trying for a long time to gather enough tiny wee ones of the same kind of shell to make one for me. I have never had a real necklace of my own before, although Kopiolani

Samoa

has often made me one from the different gorgeous flowers that grow so abundantly on all hands in Samoa. To-day she is very lucky, for the strongly running seas have brought immense quantities of shells with them, and debris of all kinds, and she is continually stooping down and picking up another and another, as her sharp eyes spot them lying on the sand. At last the tide comes in so far that all the girls have to return to the spot from which they were surf-riding, and by this time the sun has completely dried their hair and bodies, so that they can proceed to dress. Samoa is a land of continual summer, so that much clothing would be unnecessary, and the girls all wear a skirt that extends from the shoulders to the knees, just the same way that my own dress does. Although I have told you so much of the playtime doings, you must not suppose that Kopiolani does nothing but play, for she has to go to school and perform many other duties.

For instance, there is water to be fetched, and this is carried in very remarkable bottles made from cocoanut shells. First of all, a small hole is cut in the top of the nut, and then a number of sharp stones are put inside, and the nut shaken and shaken until all the soft kernel is removed. A cork to stop the hole is then made, from banana leaves rolled tightly together. Often and often I have been with Kopiolani to the stream with a

Peeps at the World's Dolls

string of these quaint bottles to fill, and as we return she generally picks a flower to stick in her hair, and then one for me. As we come home, she sings, all the way, a lovely "Sleep, Dolly," song, so that at last, when the darkness falls and we are ready to go to bed, we are both as sleepy, as sleepy can be.

CHAPTER XVIII

HOLLAND

SOME people have a very strange idea, when you speak to them about a Dutch doll, and think that we are all made of wood, with thin arms and legs that work upon wooden pegs, and that our heads are nearly round, with black painted hair and eyebrows, with a dab of vivid carmine upon each cheek. Nothing could be further from the truth. Dutch dollies—real Dutch dollies, that is—are quite as varied and beautiful as those of any other country, and our little mistresses certainly take quite as much care of us, and spend even more time in dressing and playing with us than English girls do.

Of course, my name is Wilhelmina, one of the best names for a loyal Dutch girl, and I live a very happy life in my lowland home where everything

Holland

is kept so neat and clean, and where, especially in the spring months of the year, there is so much vivid colour and beauty to be seen. But before I tell you anything at all about my country or its beauties, let me tell you how I am dressed, and what I look like. My face is more " square " and flat than your English dolly, but really there is not much difference in us, for my eyes are blue and my hair very fair, and I am made of " biscuit " china, so that my whole expression is very live and vivacious.

My clothes are far more bulky than yours; it is not at all Dutch to look slim, so that I wear quantities and quantities of petticoats, which give me my plump appearance. On my head I wear the Dutch bonnet or cap, made of white muslin, fitting tightly to my head, but which has also two side wings that stand out on either side of my face and are stiffly starched. My bodice is tight, but the sleeves only reach to the elbow, and under this is a chemisette of white, embroidered in colour, and round my neck a string of coral beads. As I told you, my skirt is very full, and over it I have an apron without a bib.

Of course, my feet are shod with clogs; everywhere you go in Holland you will hear the clitter-clatter of clogs over the cobbled streets, and my own feet are no exception to the rule. Can you picture at all the kind of home in which we live, I wonder, and

Peeps at the World's Dolls

the life we live ? Betje—that is the name of my little mistress—is the daughter of a bulb farmer, and our house is long and low with a bright red roof, and adjoining it is a large storehouse where dozens of men and girls are always at work, sorting and cleaning and packing the bulbs that are sent all over the world to beautify the spring garden. Everywhere you can see the windmills, which are always at work, pumping and pumping to keep the land dry.

I have not been played with much lately, for Betje has been ill, but now she is better and sitting up in her bed again, and the first thing she asked for was me. She cannot sit up for long together yet, and so she has propped me up at her feet so that I can see out of the window and tell her all that is happening outside. And what do I see ? A wide stretch of perfectly flat country, spreading for miles and miles as far as ever I can imagine; but this, of course, is no interest to Betje, she wants to hear about the things near to home.

First, there is the canal that comes almost up to the house door at the side. This is a very curious canal, for so much of our land is below the level of the sea that our canals are higher than the land through which they run, and therefore the banks are mounded up higher than the fields through which they flow.

"Yes, Betje ! There is quite a large ship just

Holland

outside, and Johann is leaning over the side, talking to the sailor-men who are idling about on the deck. The mate is leaning against the mast, and has a broad smile upon his face at some remark Johann has made."

And now I look out across the fields and the stables, where Pieter is sanding the floor for the horses and cattle. What a sea of colour! The last of the daffodils are still filling their squares with primrose yellow and gold, for all the ground is set out in squares, each filled with one kind of bulb, so that the whole looks like a giant draught-board painted in many different colours. Those squares of vivid blue, pink, red, white, and purple, are fields of hyacinths, and as the curtain flaps with the soft wind one can smell nothing but the powerful fragrance of hundreds of thousands of the stiff spikes of flower, set in rows just like a regiment of soldiers.

Everywhere Dutch girls and women and men are at work among the flowers, and, as I tell Betje about it all, she longs to be up and out with the rest of the world, revelling in the sun and fragrant blossom. Presently her mother comes in with a glass of milk that she must drink, and in her other hand a gorgeous bunch of the first tulips and some blue muscari. The milk is drunk, Betje lies down " comfy " again, I am put into her arms, and we both go off to sleep; so that it may not be many days ere we are both out in the air again, amongst all the other girls and boys, laughing and playing among the fields of fragrant blossom in the happy spring flower-time—a Dutch doll and a Dutch girl in a typical piece of Nederland.

CHAPTER XIX

TURKEY

I THINK that, among the various dollies that have appeared in this book, I must look one of the most remarkable, and I certainly have had a very adventurous life. I began life in a factory in France, where thousands and thousands of other dolls—just like myself—were made every year. From there I was sent to a shop and displayed in the window, just in the same way as every other dolly begins life. I saw the usual sights: people—men and women, boys and girls—passing by, the carts and motor-cars in the streets, and all the things with which Europeans are so familiar.

And then, one day, a lady came into the shop and bought me, with three or four of my sisters. I do not know where she came from, because I could not understand a word that she said; but we were all packed away in a box, and I saw nothing more until I awoke in a strange place among

Turkey

strange people, where everything was quite different to anything I had ever seen or imagined. I had to learn to understand a new language, wear new clothes, and live an entirely new kind of life. It was almost like a miracle to me, because, you see, I am a sleeping doll, and all the while I was lying down in the box my eyes were tightly shut, and so I knew nothing. And then I woke— will you believe me ?—in the harem of a Turkish home. The lady, who had bought me in the French shop was there, a number of other women, and quite a lot of children. I just opened my eyes in one big stare when I was held upright. The lady was holding me out towards a bright-eyed and attractive little girl with masses of dark hair, and never before have I seen so much wonder in a pair of human eyes as shone from those of Fatme (as, I found, she was called). Could it be possible that this great and wonderful doll was for her—all her very own self ? Little girls are of but small account in Turkey, and no one ever thinks of giving them presents in the form of toys. Young as she was, Fatme had quite a considerable amount of jewellery which her father had bought for her; for from the time she was four years old her father had been buying her various gold and other ornaments so that, when she grew up, she would have a rich supply wherewith to tempt a possible husband; but dolls or toys—oh, no !

Peeps at the World's Dolls

And then I came—brought by this wonderful lady from a wonderful foreign land, and allowed to enter the harem as a special favour. No wonder that Fatme could not believe the evidence of those bright, shining eyes of hers. And that is how I became a Turkish lady, living out my whole life in seclusion and wearing the strange dress of a country quite different to my own.

After my first surprise, when I had time to look round, I saw that all the women and girls wore short skirts that barely reached to their knees, under which was a very large number of other skirts or petticoats, showing that I was in a very fashionable household indeed; for the more skirts, the higher the rank of the woman. All their legs were bare, though slippers with high heels were generally worn, and the top of the body was covered by a short, loose jacket with long, tight sleeves. This bodice was open down the front and highly decorated.

Almost everyone wore a handkerchief on the head, and two of the girls had an aigrette as well. But the most curious thing of all was that everybody, except the very smallest girls, wore a thin veil over the face. It took me a long time to get used to such a queer life, where no one ever seemed to do anything, because there were so many girls to wait upon you, and one rarely, if ever, went out.

Turkey

Fatme, after spending several days in doing nothing but gazing at me in wonder, began to make me a set of clothes exactly as those I have described above, and when I got used to them I began to feel much more at home. One of the most curious things of all to me was that there seemed to be no men in the country, or I never saw any; but day after day we lived the same life in the harem, never going out of doors, and surrounded only by the children and girls who waited upon us.

But a day came when I was to get a glimpse more of my new land, though, as you will agree, it was but a glimpse. For we went out—a rare and unusual event. Everything that I had just begun to grow accustomed to was changed by this, for we all had to put on an entirely new set of garments. These consisted of three pieces: a pair of trousers, a "chuddar," and a long veil. The trousers were very wide, and over these the large black "chuddar," then the veil, which consisted of a strip of white calico with openwork for the eyes, and which was fastened at the back of the head with a gold brooch. I did not like this at all, but all the girls seemed to think it just a matter of course, as soon as they are over ten years old, and all that we met were dressed in exactly the same way. The men walk the streets uncovered, and many of them wear great dark beards, and take

Peeps at the World's Dolls

no notice at all of any of the women and children that they pass.

It is a beautiful and wonderful country, with its unusual buildings and mosques, and I love to be here with my dear Fatme; but never, never, never will it seem other than strange, when I think of France, and the days before I became a Turkish dolly.

CHAPTER XX

A MONGOLIAN LADY AND A MANCHU GENTLEMAN

DID you ever see two more curious dolls than the Mongolian lady and the Manchu gentleman that are shown in colour on the opposite page? There is no need for me to tell you much about them, for you can see for yourself the splendid silks and charming colours in which they are dressed. Chinese dollies are certainly amongst the most wonderful of all the world's dolls, and remarkable copies of the living people that they represent.

Almost every phase of Chinese life is shown by these dolls, and if you were a Chinese girl it is quite possible that you might have one dressed as a farmer as he appears when walking in his rice fields. And a very curious fellow he looks too,

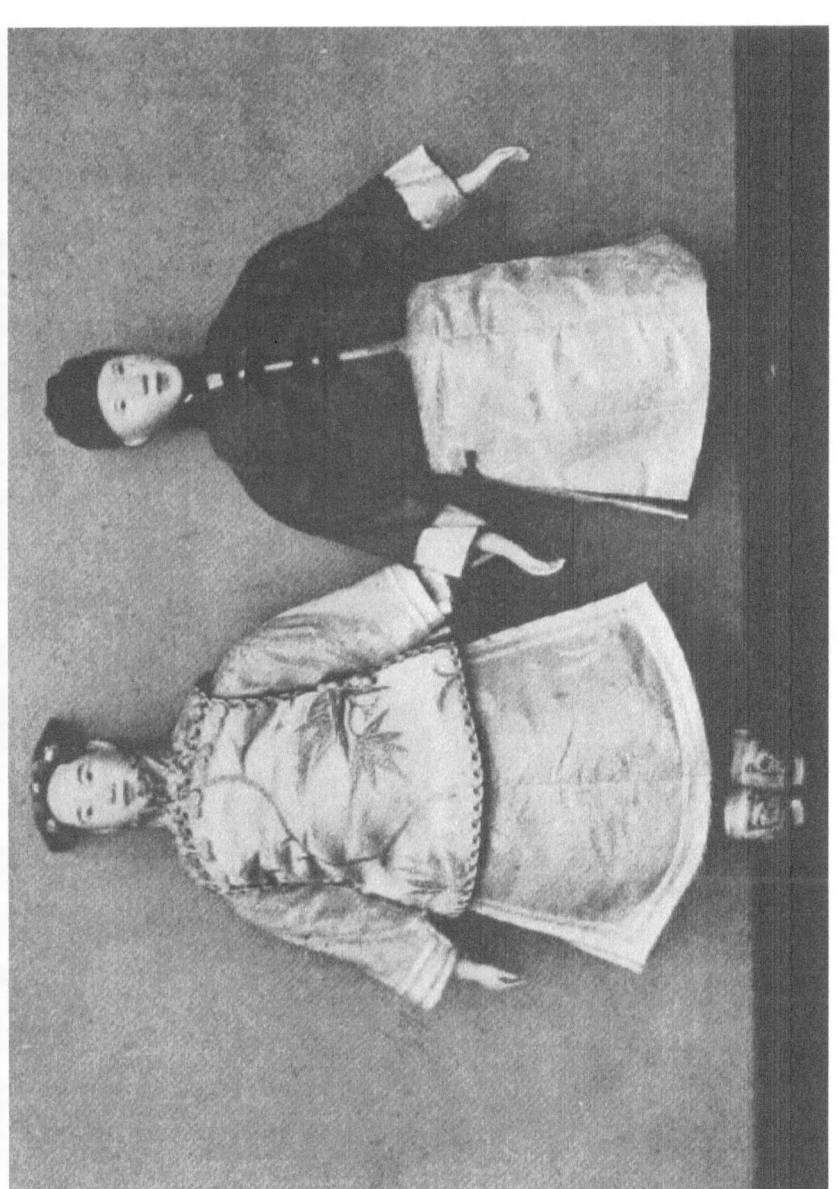

MONGOLIAN DOLLS.
Representing a lady and a gentleman.

A Mongolian and a Manchu

with his straw garments and big straw hat. He wears no shoes upon his feet, because he is always working in the wet fields; for rice always grows in fields that are soaking wet, and shoes would quickly be ruined.

Two more unusual Chinese dolls that I should like to tell you about are the widow and chief mourner. When a man dies, the widow mourns most extravagantly, and at the funeral she cannot show too many signs of her grief. The clothes worn, both by the widow and the chief mourner, are made of hemp, and strange hats are placed upon the head. That of the chief mourner is the most remarkable of the two, for in the front are three large tears that are as big as oranges, and which are bought with the hat.

Dolls just exactly like these can be bought in the shops, and you would be greatly surprised at the marvellous modelling and colouring of the faces and limbs. Everything about them is perfect, even down to each tiny finger and toe. Years ago it used to be the custom to bind the feet of the better-class Chinese girls so that they could not grow very big; the smaller the feet, the more beautiful she was considered to be, and I have seen a wee Chinese dolly with the tiniest feet, and correspondingly tiny shoes splendidly embroidered in varicoloured silks. A poor, pitiful little figure she looked, and one can but be

Peeps at the World's Dolls

glad that this cruel custom is now a thing of the past, although dollies are still made to show how the living girls used to be crippled.

Not only are wonderful dolls made that are exact models of live people and their clothes, but other objects are manufactured too. For instance, there is the coolie doll and his barrow. He wears short pantaloons that only just reach to the knee, a short coated tunic with a broad sash, and a twisted turban-like cap of the same colour as the sash. Pad! pad! pad! His bare feet flop over the road as he trundles his barrow in front of him. This barrow is quite different to the English one, for it has a big wheel towards the centre, and it has two feet at the back to balance it when stood down. The top of the barrow is quite flat, with two boards at the centre, so that the wheel does not rub against the baskets or whatever is being carried. Usually two large baskets are roped upon this, one on either side, and thus goods and merchandise are carried from place to place.

One of the most showy Chinese dolls is the girl bride; and how very different she appears to our own English girl who is going to be married! Brilliant colour and embroidery are a great feature, including the shoes, which are simply one mass of finely worked silk. Down the front of the skirt hangs a kind of apron, gorgeous in gold and silver embroi-

A Mongolian and a Manchu

dery, the sleeves of the coat being similarly decorated. On her head she wears a cap upon which beads and strings of beads are lavishly used, with a covering for the face that comes nearly to the waist, and over which strings of pearl beads are hung. Her hands are most carefully concealed, it being the height of bad manners for these to be shown.

Of the more common dolls that the girls play with, there is a great distinction in the way they are dressed according to the age they are supposed to be. A young girl doll would not have a skirt, but a pair of silk trousers reaching to the ankles, while she wears a piece of her hair loose and hanging over the right shoulder. Should she be a young lady, however, her hair would be gathered up beneath a close-fitting cap; instead of the trousers, she would wear a long skirt, from beneath which only her toes, with their tiny shoes, would show.

In Central China, where they are less civilised, dolls are nothing like so good as those I have described to you, and are but crude representations indeed. One that is very common is made of china, a squatting figure with a round head and funny little short arms. The head is the most life-like part of it, and the whole is decorated in different coloured paints, then burned and glazed. There is nothing lovable at all about it, but the other

Peeps at the World's Dolls

and earlier described dolls are certainly as perfect as anything that is made in the most up-to-date European factory.

CHAPTER XXI

BELGIUM, THE GREAT ADVENTURE

AH! What was that? A loud crash, and a nearer boom than before. For two days past there had been this horrible sound in the air. Boom! boom! boom! Just like someone battering against a wall, which is exactly what it was. The armies of Germany and Austria, pounding and battering against a wall of my gallant countrymen. A wall that was to bend and give—but never break, until the forces of destruction had been utterly and completely defeated.

Ghislaine, my little owner, was too young to understand all this, and she gazed with wondering eyes at the crowds that thronged the roadway all day and half the night. A crowd fleeing from the terror that pressed hard upon their heels. A crowd of women, children, boys, girls, and—yes, dolls too; for everyone carried some small article that was precious, so that you may be sure that the girls did not leave their dollies behind. Presently our turn came too, and we were ordered

Belgium, the Great Adventure

to retire from the village which had hitherto been the only bit of the world we had known. Poor, peaceful little village! I had but a small idea of how long it would be before I saw it again, or to what a condition it would have been brought. Ghislaine's mother grabbed her up, she herself grabbed me, and I am sure that none of us have the least idea how we did reach the coast.

Here, too, the confusion was indescribable, and no one seemed to have the smallest notion of where we were to go, or what we were to do. At last, however, we were hustled on to a ship that was to carry us to England, the country over the sea of which I had only heard the name. Ghislaine cuddled me very close to her, for she is a wonderful little mother, although I think she was nearly as frightened as I was. We had no room to move, so tightly were we packed, and when night came no one dared show the least glimpse of light. It was awful, and I expected every moment that we should all find ourselves in the sea, upon which the ship tossed and rolled in such an alarming way.

I could not sleep, because my eyes are not the kind that are made to shut, and all through that dreadful night I stared around me at the pitiful crowd; but Ghislaine slept soundly in her mother's arms, utterly tired out. A wee, wistful child. Truly " He giveth His beloved sleep."

Peeps at the World's Dolls

And then Folkestone, with all the busy landing, where we were greeted by smiling faces and outstretched arms. Ghislaine cried when a lady took her from her mother's arms, and she clung tightly to me as we were given milk and food before being put into the London train.

Through miles and miles—and miles again—of countryside we steamed, showing no traces of the horror that was behind us, save that everywhere were the khaki boys, that through long years were to stand side by side with us and suffer and die. God bless them—every one! God bless England, and may we neither of us ever forget that we are brothers indeed!

But I must hurry on with my story. A home was found, and nobody seemed as if they could do enough for me. Much that happened I did not at all understand; for, although I knew everything that Ghislaine and her mother talked of, it was a long time before I grew to know the language of the English. Many details of our life and home I shall omit, but you must hear the tale of the new doll. Everybody loved Ghislaine at once, and before many weeks had passed by the ladies who used to visit us in our hostel made her the greatest pet of all the children there, and especially because she loved and played with me very contentedly for so many hours of each day. It all seemed very strange, I can tell you. Just a little

Belgium, the Great Adventure

bit of Belgium, cut out and planted down in another land where one heard the "vlaamigen" spoken in the streets almost every time we went out.

Then came your wonderful Christmas, with its games and laughter, when, once again, all the ladies did everything that they could to make life good to us strangers. When Ghislaine woke up on Christmas morning, what do you think she saw? Hanging on the corner of her cot at the foot, a stocking, very fat and big, bulging out in the queerest lumps and corners. Up she scrambled to see whatever this might mean, and there, inside that stocking, was the most wonderful treasure-house of good things, including a wonderful new dolly that positively opened and shut her eyes. For just a moment I did feel jealous, and then I looked at Ghislaine's face to see what she thought of it. Just as though she knew what I was feeling, she smiled at me as I sat on the end of the cot, reached out her hand, and gave me one mighty cuddle that soon told me I was second to nobody in her affection. Yes, the new dolly, brilliant with wax face, might open and shut her eyes, but I—I—I was *the* dolly that held her heart. Since then I have grown to be ashamed of my jealous feeling, not alone because Ghislaine was so loyal a little soul and stood by her first love, but because the English doll is such a good sort, and

Peeps at the World's Dolls

we live together the happiest and most perfect friends: a sign, let us hope, of the feeling that will ever endure between our races.

Yes, the new doll was clothed and played with and cuddled just the same as I was, so that she too could have no feeling of neglect.

So the years went by, and with startling suddenness came Armistice Day and the succession of events that led to peace again, and we Belgians had proved above everything else that, though we had sacrificed much, we had retained that which counts above all else—our soul.

And then, one day, we set out upon the last stage of our great adventure—the return home. For, good as England had been to us; much as she had given with both hands, one thing she could not provide—the little Belgium, our native land.

Memories of you are very sweet and pleasant, and I am glad that I, a Belgian dolly, should have grown to know you and your English life so well, but for me always it is the little Belgium.

And so we returned again to our village home, sadly torn and wrecked by the ravages of war, but still the best place on earth—Home! I was especially nice to the English dolly for many weeks after our return, for I knew exactly how it felt to be quite alone among strangers, and many other little Belgian girls, beside Ghislaine, have

A Midsummer Night's Dream

played with the wonderful doll that came from over the sea with us and can go to sleep when she is laid down.

Henri was not killed, although he is very lame in one leg; but now that we are all together again, what does that matter beside the many who gave up the greatest thing of all—their life?

And so ends my Great Adventure.

CHAPTER XXII

A MIDSUMMER NIGHT'S DREAM

So we come to the last chapter on the World's Dolls. And everything that I am now going to tell you happened only the last night that ever was. It is no good telling me that it was just a dream! Nothing of the sort!

It is true that I was asleep when it began, true that I went to sleep again afterwards; but that all that happened was just a dream—nonsense! Nonsense!! I tell you I was awake and saw it all, so what more can you want?

The first thing that woke me was a boom. Someone had loudly struck a drum. Then again—boom! boom! By this time I was sitting bolt upright in my bed with the eiderdown gathered round my shoulders.

Peeps at the World's Dolls

Boom! boom! Again the drum, and then the trumpets and flutes, tra-tra-la-la-la-tra-la-la-la-laaa——

No, there was no mistake; it was the orchestra in a theatre, just before the curtain rang up for the last scene of the pantomine. Silence! A faint ting! ting! ting! Out broke the orchestra with a will: flutes, violins, drums, trumpets, piano—faster and faster, louder and louder, until with a final crash, in which both drum and cymbals seemed to be seeing which could outdo the other, the music came to a pause.

Everything, until now, had been in complete darkness, but—will you believe it?—as I sat there in bed, the big wardrobe (of which I could faintly see the looking-glass) slowly rolled to one side, just like the safety curtain rolls up, and there, before my eyes, was a miniature stage, brilliantly lit, and backed by gay scenery. No one could be seen, but there were tall palm trees waving in the background, a sea, as blue as blue, a flight of steps in front leading down from a Moorish palace to the stage.

As I watched, more and more scenery seemed to roll away, and I could see further and further out to sea, where a big ship in the distance was making its way towards the shore. Then, softly and drowsily, the orchestra began to play flutes and violins, and a wee figure tripped upon the

A Midsummer Night's Dream

fairy stage. What a start I had, for there, before my very eyes, was the English dolly, one hundred years old, with her crinoline, red cloak, and blue ribboned bonnet, just as you see her on the first page of this book, For all the weight of her years, she moved like a girl, and, after bowing towards me, she went across the stage and sat down upon a flowery bank near the entrance to the Moorish palace towards the sea. And then things began to happen so fast that I can scarcely tell you of them quickly enough.

From either side of the stage English dollies, of every kind that you can possibly imagine, began to pour in. There were soldier dolls, sailor dolls, hospital nurses, round chubby baby dolls, young ladies, pedlars, Quaker girls, country girls, Little Lord Fauntleroys, Thumbs-ups, Woolly-heads, Golliwogs, even Teddy-bears and Penguins, until it looked as if there would not be room for another one to find a place. But each one fell into his or her own particular spot at the side and left the centre quite clear.

The music by now had grown quite loud again, and as I watched I saw that the great ship which had been so far across the sea was drawing nearer and nearer, until, just as she grounded upon the shore, the orchestra broke out into " Rule, Britannia ":

"Britons never, never shall be slaves."

Peeps at the World's Dolls

I took my eyes from the brilliant scene for just a moment to look at the orchestra. Yes, there was a miniature conductor, frantically waving his hand and baton as he conducted, and really I thought the little fellow with the drum would have burst it and himself too, so lustily did he whack at it when he came to the final bar. Then, back to the stage again!

Forward sprang the bluejackets and the soldiers and caught the ropes, which the other sailor dollies on board flung to them, and then I looked at the crowd on board, waiting to land. The ropes were secured in a trice, and the sailors, flinging their caps down, prepared to steady the gangway that was being lowered from the ship to the shore. All this time the orchestra was silent, as though waiting for a cue; it came when the gangway was safely lashed in position.

The English doll rose from her seat; the conductor tapped with his baton, and down the gangway (just as I told you in the second chapter), stepped little Miss America, while the orchestra played "The Star-Spangled Banner." Ere she had quite reached the shore, a Japanese boy began to descend, and again the orchestra changed to appropriate music.

In rapid succession the passengers streamed off: Russia, Lapland, Italy, Hungary, France (of course, with "La Marseillaise"), Norway, Sunny Spain,

A Midsummer Night's Dream

Switzerland, Holland, Belgium ("La Brabançonne," Mr. Orchestra, please!), Turkish girls closely veiled, until you would never have believed it possible that the ship could have held so many. Finally the Captain and the crew followed, and there were only two or three men left on board, grinning broadly as they hung over the side.

Surely, I thought, this is the end; but, almost before I had had time to think it, the door of the Moorish palace was flung open, the orchestra recommenced, and down the steps came the Flathead dolly, just as I have described her to you. Really, it was too ridiculous to see (actually see!) all these dollies walking off the ship and down the steps, just like live things. The door did not shut behind her, and I caught a dazzling vision of the Precious Child of Korea, as she made her way rather totteringly down the steps. Then came the Samoan girl, the queer little Kaffir clay doll, and crowds and crowds of others of every nationality under the sun. When the ugly little Kaffir doll appeared, several others broke into a peal of laughter at her quaint appearance, and it was just here that the sailor-boys showed how fine they are all through; for, while some of the others were beginning to laugh, one stepped forward, and, with a bow, took her arm, and, with his head in the air, walked down the steps, courteous and proud as any king.

Peeps at the World's Dolls

Hurrah, sailor-boy! I did clap that, you may be sure.

But what is happening now? The orchestra has stopped! Out go all the lights, and it is night! A monotonous dub! dub! dub! on the small drum, gradually getting faster and faster.

Suddenly the blackness is pierced by a brilliant beam of light from the ship: they have put on a searchlight, which creeps across the sea feeling and feeling its way. For what? Ah!—a great gasp of wonder! The searchlight has steadied, and there its beam is concentrated upon a tiny silvery aeroplane—no, two! No, there are half a dozen of them, winging their way across the black night. Even as we watch another marvel is happening, and the sun peeps, the edge of his golden disc above the edge of the sea, joining his rays to that of the searchlight. First pink, then red, then gold, then yellow, until the shadowy figures upon the stage become quite clear again and everything is illumined by bright, radiant light. Now the first of the aeroplanes is circling round and round as it descends, gracefully as a bird, to the stage.

And who can be inside it? We have not long to wait, for out steps Miss Serbia (too late to catch the boat). The second comes to earth with a tail-spin: Rip Van Winkle has arrived, and he is awake too, wide awake! Number three reaches the stage, and out steps the Schoolmaster, with a

A Midsummer Night's Dream

little skull cap and glasses through which he peers enquiringly at the scene around him. His waistcoat is white, he wears a velveteen coat and no birch is in his hand, only a kindly smile on his face as he gazes at the merry throng surrounding him. Everyone gives a hearty cheer, and, ere this has died away, the fourth 'plane grounds, and Miss Madeira steps forth. A queer little figure she looks, too, with her bulky legs and striped print dress, and her hair carried up to a stiff point. From the windows of the fifth aeroplane two faces can be seen—dusky faces and black hair decorated with gay feathers—an Indian chief and his squaw. Look at their moccasins as they step down, he bravely, she timidly.

Who are the passengers in the last? The Banana boy and girl. Thunders of applause greet them, for, even before they reach the ground, they begin to scatter handfuls of the fruit that they have brought with them from far-off Bermuda. What a quaint little pair of figures they make as they step from the tiny 'plane, their funny little nut heads waggling, waggling, waggling as they walk. The Banana girl holds a chic little sunshade in her hand, and the Banana boy wears a funny little hat that makes him look exactly like Charlie Chaplin.

These are the final arrivals, and the orchestra recommences another gay tune. And now every-

Peeps at the World's Dolls

body that could possibly find standing-room is crowded upon the stage. Dolls from the North, dolls from the South, dolls from the East, dolls from the West, and so to the final tableau of all the nations. Britain in the centre, behind her the good old Union Jack; France, with the tricolour; Belgium, black, yellow and red; Japan, the land of the Rising Sun; colour massed upon colour, brilliant dresses, gay flags, tuneful music working up and up to the climax. And then everyone began to chant in chorus:

> We are dollies, from all the world
> Far away over the sea;
> To-night we are holding a carnival here—
> A fête night of joyous glee.
>
> Just for to-night, we have escaped,
> Free from worry and care—
> Dollies, let loose from the stage of life
> To the Land of Anywhere.
>
> Jappies and Chappies and gay Chinese,
> Black girls and white boys, too,
> Africans, Indians, Mexicans,
> With lasses from Timbuctoo.
>
> So join in our merriment—hip, hip! Hooray!
> Sing hey for the Dolly Show!
> It's the brightest, cheeriest, merriest thing,
> Crammed full of vigour and go.
>
> Here's to all who love us so well,
> Big girls, great girls, and small.
> May you never lose the love that you have,
> For we love you, one and all!

A Midsummer Night's Dream

And then, suddenly, everything went dark, and I shivered. A dream? Nothing of the kind! It is true that, when I woke in the morning with the sunlight streaming through the blind, the wardrobe was back in its place as though it had never been moved. You may be sure I did move it, in my endeavour to find the mystic Dolly Show. The paper was on the wall, and, although I tapped and tapped, I could not find any hollow-sounding place. But I know that the wardrobe did roll away. I know that the dollies were there. I know that I did sit up in bed, wrapped in the eiderdown; and anyone who says again that it's a dream—well, poof for your dream, so there!

www.ingramcontent.com/pod-product-compliance
Lightning Source LLC
Chambersburg PA
CBHW020234170426
43201CB00007B/422